OMAHA BEACH

D0645216

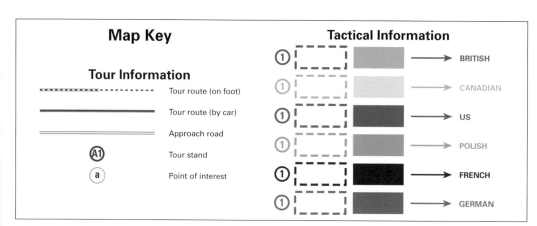

Map Key

Tour Information

▪▪▪▪▪▪▪▪---------- Tour route (on foot)

——————————— Tour route (by car)

═══════════════ Approach road

(A1) Tour stand

(a) Point of interest

Tactical Information

① [- - - -] ▨ ⟶ **BRITISH**

① [- - - -] ▨ ⟶ CANADIAN

① [- - - -] ▨ ⟶ **US**

① [- - - -] ▨ ⟶ POLISH

① [- - - -] ▨ ⟶ **FRENCH**

① [- - - -] ▨ ⟶ **GERMAN**

OMAHA BEACH

STEPHEN BADSEY & TIM BEAN

The
History
Press

While every effort has been made to ensure that the information given in this book is accurate, the publishers, the author and the series editor do not accept responsibility for any errors or omissions or for any changes in the details given in this guide or for the consequence of any reliance on the information provided. The publishers would be grateful if readers would advise them of any inaccuracies they may encounter so these can be considered for future editions of this book.

The inclusion of any place to stay, place to eat, tourist attraction or other establishment in this book does not imply an endorsement or recommendation by the publisher, the series editor or the author. Their details are included for information only. Directions are for guidance only and should be used in conjunction with other sources of information.

Front cover: Infantrymen land on Omaha Beach's Easy Red sector, 0730 hours, 6 June 1944. (US National Archives [USNA])

Page 1: A 155-mm gun barrel, part of the memorial at the Pointe du Hoc. *(Simon Trew [SCT])*

Page 3: Troops of 5th Engineer Special Brigade disembark late on the afternoon of 6 June. *(USNA)*

Page 7: The inexorable tide rolls on. US Landing Ships Tank discharge their cargoes across the sands of Omaha Beach, while a mass of merchant shipping awaits its turn offshore. *(USNA)*

First published 2004 as part of the Battle Zone Normandy series
This edition published 2011

The History Press
The Mill, Brimscombe Port
Stroud, Gloucestershire, GL5 2QG
www.thehistorypress.co.uk

© Stephen Badsey & Tim Bean, 2004, 2011
Tour base maps © Institute Géographique National, Paris
GSGS (1944) base maps © The British Library/Crown Copyright

The right of Stephen Badsey & Tim Bean to be identified as
the authors of this work has been asserted in accordance with the
Copyrights, Designs and Patents Act 1988.

All rights reserved. No part of this book may be reprinted
or reproduced or utilised in any form or by any electronic,
mechanical or other means, now known or hereafter invented,
including photocopying and recording, or in any information
storage or retrieval system, without the permission in writing
from the Publishers.

British Library Cataloguing in Publication Data.
A catalogue record for this book is available from the British Library.

ISBN 978 0 7524 5915 8

Typesetting and origination by The History Press
Manufacturing managed by Jellyfish Print Solutions Ltd.
Printed in India

CONTENTS

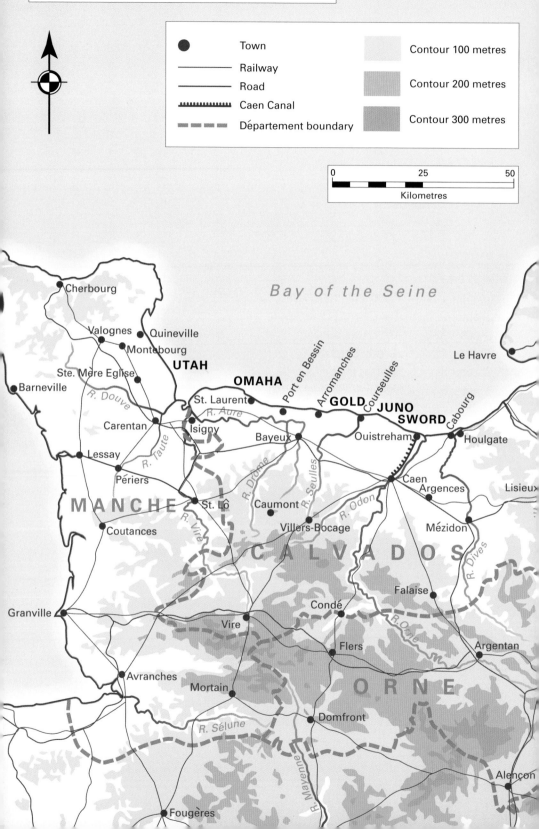

THE NORMANDY BATTLEFIELD

●	Town
——	Railway
——	Road
▛▜▛▜	Caen Canal
– – –	Département boundary

Contour 100 metres
Contour 200 metres
Contour 300 metres

0   25   50
Kilometres

Bay of the Seine

Cherbourg

Valognes Quineville
Montebourg
Ste. Mère Eglise   UTAH
Barneville   OMAHA
R. Douve   Port en Bessin Arromanches   Le Havre
St. Laurent   Courseulles
Carentan Isigny   R. Aure   GOLD JUNO
Bayeux   SWORD   Cabourg
Lessay   Ouistreham   Houlgate
R. Taute   Caen
Périers   R. Drôme   Argences   Lisieux
MANCHE   St. Lô   Caumont   R. Seulles   R. Odon
Coutances   Villers-Bocage   Mézidon
R. Vire   CALVADOS   R. Dives
Falaise
Condé
Granville   Vire   R. Orne
Flers   Argentan
Avranches   ORNE
Mortain
R. Sélune   Domfront
R. Mayenne   Alençon
Fougères

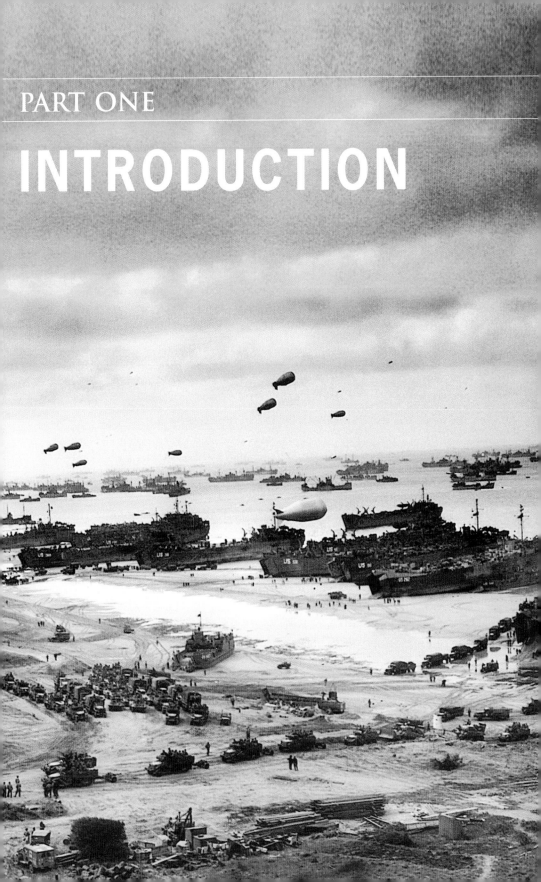

PART ONE

INTRODUCTION

BATTLE ZONE NORMANDY

The Battle of Normandy was one of the greatest military clashes of all time. From late 1943, when the Allies appointed their senior commanders and began the air operations that were such a vital preliminary to the invasion, until the end of August 1944, it pitted against one another several of the most powerful nations on earth, as well as some of their most brilliant minds. When it was won, it changed the world forever. The price was high, but for anybody who values the principles of freedom and democracy, it is difficult to conclude that it was one not worth paying.

I first visited Lower Normandy in 1994, a year after I joined the War Studies Department at the Royal Military Academy Sandhurst (RMAS). With the 50th anniversary of D-Day looming, it was decided that the British Army would be represented at several major ceremonies by one of the RMAS's officer cadet companies. It was also suggested that the cadets should visit some of the battlefields, not least to bring home to them the significance of why they were there. Thus, at the start of June 1994, I found myself as one of a small team of military and civilian directing staff flying with the cadets in a draughty and noisy Hercules transport to visit the beaches and fields of Calvados, in my case for the first time.

I was hooked. Having met some of the veterans and seen the ground over which they fought – and where many of their friends died – I was determined to go back. Fortunately, the Army encourages battlefield touring as part of its soldiers' education, and on numerous occasions since 1994 I have been privileged to return to Normandy, often to visit new sites. In the process I have learned a vast amount, both from my colleagues (several of whom are contributors to this series) and from my enthusiastic and sometimes tri-service audiences, whose professional insights and penetrating questions have frequently made me re-examine my own assumptions and prejudices. Perhaps inevitably, especially when standing in one of Normandy's beautifully-maintained Commonwealth War Graves Commission cemeteries, I have also found myself deeply moved by the critical events that took place there in the summer of 1944.

The hardback 'Battle Zone Normandy' series (now published in paperback with the series motif 'D-Day') was originally conceived by Jonathan Falconer, Commissioning Editor at Sutton Publishing, in 2001. Why not, he suggested, bring together recent academic research – some of which challenges the general perception of what happened on and after 6 June 1944 – with a perspective based on familiarity with the ground itself? We agreed that the opportunity existed for a series that would set out to combine detailed and accurate narratives, based mostly on primary sources, with illustrated guides to the ground itself, which could be used either in the field (sometimes quite literally), or by the armchair explorer. The book in your hands is the product of that agreement.

The series consisted of 14 volumes, covering most of the major and many of the minor engagements that went together to create the Battle of Normandy. The first six books deal with the airborne and amphibious landings on 6 June 1944, and with the struggle to create the firm lodgement that was the prerequisite for eventual Allied victory. Five further volumes cover some of the critical battles that followed, as the Allies' plans unravelled and they were forced to improvise a battle very different from that originally intended. Finally, the last three titles in the series examine the fruits of the bitter attritional struggle of June and July 1944, as the Allies irrupted through the German lines or drove them back in fierce fighting. The series ends, logically enough, with the devastation of the German armed forces in the 'Falaise Pocket' in late August.

Whether you use these books while visiting Normandy, or to experience the battlefields vicariously, we hope you will find them as interesting to read as we did to research and write. Far from the inevitable victory that is sometimes represented, D-Day and the ensuing battles were full of hazards and unpredictability. Contrary to the view often expressed, had the invasion failed, it is far from certain that a second attempt could have been mounted. Remember this, and the significance of the contents of this book, not least for your life today, will be the more obvious.

Dr Simon Trew
Royal Military Academy Sandhurst
December 2003

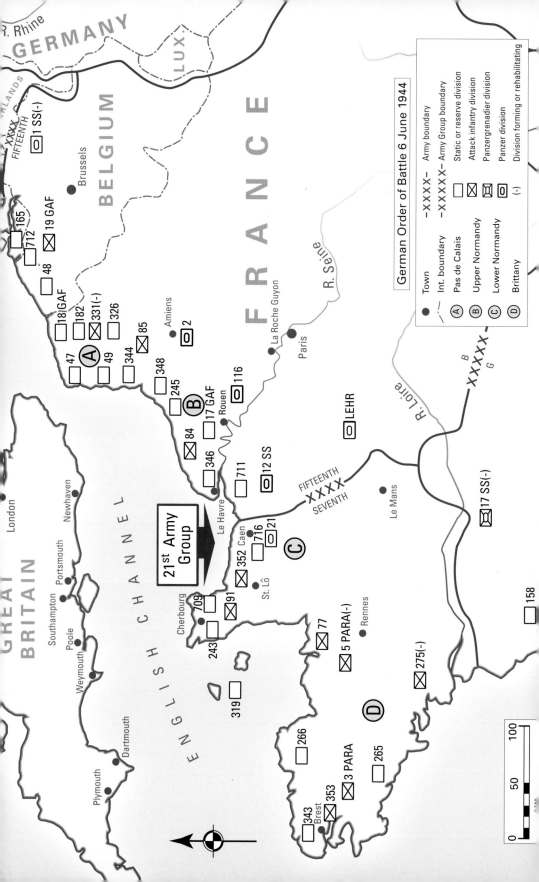

PART TWO

HISTORY

CHAPTER 1

PLANS AND PREPARATIONS

Page 11: Into the maelstrom. Troops of 1/16th RCT wade ashore on Easy Red sector, some time between 0730 and 0800 hours, 6 June 1944. Smoke from burning grass helped to hide their landing from the German defenders on the bluffs in the background. However, many casualties were sustained as the battalion attempted to advance inland. *(USNA)*

Along the Calvados coast of Lower Normandy in the Bay of the Seine, almost exactly half-way between the two major ports of Le Havre to the east and Cherbourg to the west, lies a beautiful expanse of firm yellow sand, framed on either side by steep cliffs and backed by high hills or bluffs. Known before the Second World War as la Plage d'Or ('the golden beach'), on D-Day, Tuesday 6 June 1944, this popular holiday location earned a new name, 'Omaha Beach', used ever since even by locals. It was here that the hardest fight of D-Day took place at the start of the Battle of Normandy. Just on 0630 hours, troops of the US Army's V Corps under Major General (Maj Gen) Leonard T. 'Gee' Gerow, led by 1st Infantry Division with soldiers of 29th Infantry Division, Engineers, Rangers, and US Navy sailors under its command, landed from the sea to face the Omaha bluffs and their German defenders. It was at Omaha Beach that the Allies found the strongest German defences on D-Day, where they took their heaviest casualties, and where they came closest to defeat. Only the extreme bravery and determination of the Americans, coupled with overwhelming firepower, allowed them to prevail. To the troops this was 'Bloody Omaha', a place where a military legend was born.

On 3 November 1943 Adolf Hitler signed Führer Directive 51, for the first time giving the defence of occupied western Europe priority over the war on the Eastern Front against the Soviet Union. The war was swinging against Nazi Germany, and 1944 would be its climactic year. In the Atlantic, U-boats (submarines) of the German Navy (*Kriegsmarine*) continued to suffer massive losses with almost no compensating returns against Allied shipping. Allied strategic bombing of German cities and industries, chiefly from bases in eastern England by the United States Army Air Force (USAAF) operating by day, and the Royal Air Force (RAF) Bomber Command by night, was starting to impact significantly on German weapons production, with the German Air Force (*Luftwaffe*) being forced back to defend its homeland. Having already suffered repeated defeats on the Eastern Front, the Germans expected renewed Soviet attacks in the future. In July 1943 the Italian Fascist government of Benito Mussolini, Hitler's main ally in the west, had been overthrown in a coup; in September Allied forces invaded the Italian mainland, and by November the Germans were holding a defensive line by themselves just south of Rome. But greater than all these threats was the certainty that 1944 would see a major Allied amphibious assault on German-occupied France, with the intention of breaking through into Germany itself. The decisive defeat of this invasion was Nazi Germany's chief hope for survival.

A major German weakness in defending occupied France was a divided military command structure, deliberately created by the rivalries within the Nazi state. As Germany's supreme leader, Hitler played an active part in the Battle

THEN AND NOW

Much of the Omaha Beach battlefield has not changed since 1944, including the height of hills and bluffs, the location of villages, and the paths of most of the roads. But new building has taken place, particularly holiday cottages and villas, and the roads along Omaha Beach itself. Villages and hamlets have grown and merged, some have been given new names, and many field boundaries have been removed or altered. This account describes the battlefield as it was in 1944. Major differences from the present day are explained in the section on battlefield tours. Timings are based on British Double Summer Time used by the Allies, two hours ahead of GMT and one hour ahead of local French time.

A view across
Omaha Beach,
taken from
the boundary
between Dog
Green and Dog
White sectors,
looking east. (Tim
Bean [TB])

of Normandy, including the decisions of OKW. The most important Army (*Heer*) command for the battle was OB West under *Generalfeldmarschall* (Field Marshal) Gerd von Rundstedt. This had two main subordinate formations: Army Group G defending southern France, and Army Group B defending northern France, Belgium and the Netherlands, plus a *Panzer* (armoured) reserve formed in November 1943: Panzer Group West (*Panzergruppe West*) under *General der Panzertruppe* (General of Armoured Troops) Leo Freiherr Geyr von Schweppenburg.

The Allies could not invade without control both of the English Channel and the air above the battlefield, but Rundstedt had no direct authority over Navy and Air Force units in the west, and co-operation among the services was by request rather than by order. Neither German seapower nor airpower played much part in the battle for Omaha Beach, except by their absence. The defeat of the *Kriegsmarine* on the high seas meant that Naval Group West

GERMAN HIGH COMMAND

Oberster Befelshaber der Wehrmacht
(Armed Forces Commander-in-Chief): ***Adolf Hitler***

Oberkommando der Wehrmacht (OKW)
(Armed Forces High Command) Chief of Staff: *Generalfeldmarschall* Wilhelm Keitel

Oberbefelshaber West (OB West) (Commander-in-Chief West):
   Generalfeldmarschall Gerd von Rundstedt

   Luftflotte 3 (Third Air Fleet): *Generalfeldmarschall* Hugo Sperrle

   Marinegruppenkommando West (Naval Group West): *Admiral* Theodore Krancke

   Armeegruppe B (Army Group B): *Generalfeldmarschall* Erwin Rommel

      7. Armee (Seventh Army): *Generaloberst* Friedrich Dollmann

was reduced by D-Day to a few small surface vessels based mainly at Le Havre and Cherbourg. Third Air Fleet also was reduced to ineffectiveness by an Allied air campaign begun in April 1944, based on bombing the French rail system with the object both of destroying the German ability to supply and reinforce their troops, and of forcing their fighter aircraft into a defensive battle of attrition. By D-Day Third Air Fleet had under 500 aircraft remaining ready to fly, of which fewer than one third were single-engined fighters.

Instead, the German Army based its defence on what Hitler's propagandists called the 'Atlantic Wall', a chain of coastal batteries and beach defences stretching along the coast from the Netherlands to southern France, backed by reserve forces further inland. The Navy controlled the coastal batteries up to the first Allied landings, when they would switch to Army command, while the Air Force controlled anti-aircraft guns, searchlights, and even some fighting divisions and brigades. Rundstedt's OB West headquarters also had limited authority over the divisions of the *Waffen-SS*, the Nazi Party's private army.

On 5 November 1943 Hitler appointed Field Marshal Erwin Rommel to command Special Army Group Reserve, responsible for the entire Atlantic Wall; and on 15 January 1944 also to command Army Group B, consisting of Fifteenth Army defending the direct invasion route across

US troops during pre-invasion training. Their weapon is an M2 60-mm mortar, the standard light infantry mortar, which fired a 1.36-kg high explosive round to a maximum distance of 1,800 metres. *(Imperial War Museum [IWM] AP4124)*

This photograph, taken before D-Day, provides an excellent illustration of the assault equipment worn by US troops on 6 June. The attempt to waterproof rifles by enclosing them in clear pliofilm plastic covers is particularly evident. The soldiers are wearing specially issued assault jackets and the standard M1928 pattern haversack. (USNA)

the Straits of Dover to the Pas de Calais, and Seventh Army defending Lower Normandy and Brittany. Rommel argued that, 'Our only possible defence will be at the beaches – that's where the enemy is always weakest', and that because of Allied air power the panzer reserves must be held close to the coast. Rundstedt and Geyr von Schweppenburg disagreed, believing that the panzers should be held back for a counter-attack once the Allies had committed themselves ashore. The result of a complicated compromise dictated by Hitler was that on D-Day only one panzer division was close to the Normandy landings: 21st Panzer Division, which was used against the British beaches. If even part of a panzer division had reached Omaha Beach on D-Day the result could have been very different.

Compared to the Germans, the planning and command structures of the Allies for Normandy were almost models of co-operation; as they needed to be for a multinational alliance undertaking the most complex amphibious operation in history. The code-name for the campaign was Operation 'Overlord', with the landings themselves code-named Operation 'Neptune'. The choice of Lower Normandy rather than the Pas de Calais was first made

ALLIED HIGH COMMAND

Supreme Commander Allied Expeditionary Force:
General Dwight D. Eisenhower

Deputy Supreme Commander: Air Chief Marshal Sir Arthur Tedder
Chief of Staff: Lieutenant General Walter Bedell Smith
Commander-in-Chief Allied Naval Expeditionary Force:
Admiral Sir Bertram Ramsay
Commander Allied Expeditionary Air Force:
Air Chief Marshal Sir Trafford Leigh-Mallory
Commander 21st Army Group: General Sir Bernard L. Montgomery
First US Army: Lieutenant General Omar N. Bradley
Second (British) Army: Lieutenant-General Sir Miles Dempsey

in July 1943 by COSSAC (Chief of Staff to the Supreme Allied Commander) a joint Anglo-American planning staff based in England, although extensive deception measures attempted to convince the Germans that the Allies might use the direct route, and for some time after D-Day continued to suggest that Normandy was a secondary landing. In December 1943 the American General Dwight D. Eisenhower was appointed as Supreme Allied Commander for Overlord, and his new command designated SHAEF (Supreme Headquarters Allied Expeditionary Force). Responsibility for the first phase of the Battle of Normandy including D-Day was given to the British General Sir Bernard Montgomery of 21st Army Group, who planned the land battle and commanded the first Allied forces to land, First US Army under Lieutenant General (Lt Gen) Omar N. Bradley and Second (British) Army under Lt-Gen Sir Miles Dempsey.

The plans for Operation Neptune were finalised in late May 1944, but on D-Day itself and for several days

A smiling General George C. Marshall, the US Army's Chief of Staff, shakes hands with Lt Gen Omar Bradley (*left*) on Omaha Beach, 12 June 1944. *(USNA)*

LCVPs circle during an invasion rehearsal, 7 May 1944. Such manoeuvres, which were necessary while the assault craft formed up for their run-in to the beach, contributed to a considerable amount of seasickness amongst the attacking troops on D-Day. (USNA)

afterwards there was little that senior commanders could do to influence events, and the critical decisions were made by the men on the spot.

Originally planned for 5 June, the Allied landings were to take place in the early morning on five main landing beaches over a front of more than 80 kilometres (km), preceded by extensive bombing and the dropping of paratroopers by night, and by a final shore bombardment from the sea and air. The landing frontage for 21st Army Group was divided into roughly equal halves, with First US Army landing to the west of the medieval cathedral city of Bayeux, which was 8 km inland, and Second (British) Army landing to the east, close to the regional capital city of Caen. The decision to land at Utah Beach, on the eastern side of the base of the Cotentin peninsula, as well as on the Calvados coast was made to provide the widest possible frontage for the landings, so spreading the German defences. The Allied forces included Canadians, French, Dutch, Norwegians, Belgians, Greeks, Danes, Poles, Australians, New Zealanders and Irish, and the sailors and airmen who supported the landings at Utah Beach and Omaha Beach came from many nationalities. But in terms of land forces Omaha was an all-American battle.

The beaches chosen for Second (British) Army stretched for about 24 km westward from the mouth of the River Orne north of Caen in an almost continuous ribbon of sand dotted with holiday resorts and cottages, broken only by occasional rocky promontories. From east to west these were code-named 'Sword', 'Juno' and 'Gold' Beaches by the Allies. The landings by British I Corps (including a Canadian division) at Juno and at Sword were preceded by

a British airborne division landing to the east of the Orne.
The German Navy believed that any landing in this area
was unlikely due to rocky shoals offshore, the existence of
which had an important effect on the Allied planning for
D-Day. British XXX Corps under Lt-Gen G.C. Bucknall
landed on Gold Beach, and was expected to link up swiftly
with US V Corps from Omaha. But the coast between Gold
Beach and Omaha Beach was not suitable for any landing,
the shoreline rising up into a 20 km stretch of limestone
cliffs over 30 metres (90 feet) high, with fallen rocks and
debris and only a few small stretches of sand and pebbles.
Due north of Bayeux, these cliffs were so dangerous
that the local name was 'Le Chaos', and the only breaks
were steep valleys leading to the small seaside villages of
Arromanches-les-Bains and Port-en-Bessin. Local folklore
attributed the name of the Calvados coast and region to a
corruption of *Salvador*, a galleon of the Spanish Armada of
1588 wrecked on the offshore shoals near Arromanches.

The only substantial beach along this coast was the
7,500-metre stretch of Omaha, where the cliffs drew a
short distance back from the shore to form a line of bluffs
(or low hills) 35–60 metres high, with four routes inland
through overgrown gulleys or ravines each no more than
50 metres across, known to the Americans as 'draws' from
their resemblance to the dried river-beds of the mid-western
United States. Immediately to the west the cliffs resumed with

Infantry hit the
beach during
a pre-invasion
exercise in
England. (IWM
PC10575)

The transport network inland from Omaha Beach consisted mainly of relatively narrow and poorly surfaced roads, often lined with thick hedges. Here, according to the original wartime caption, US Rangers advance past French civilians towards their objective along one such road. Photograph taken on 7 June. (USNA)

the Pointe et Raz de la Percée headland (called the Pointe de la Percée in some accounts) which blocked any direct line of sight westward towards Utah Beach. A further 4 km on was a second headland called the Pointe du Hoc (known through some long-forgotten error in US Army and Navy maps and accounts, and many since based on them, as the 'Pointe du Hoe'), followed by further breaks in the cliffs at the seaside village of Grandcamp-les-Bains and the smaller village of Maisy (later joined into Grandcamp-Maisy). Beyond these headlands, separating the Calvados coast from the Cotentin, was the flat and muddy estuary of the River Vire, also unsuitable for amphibious landings. Omaha Beach was over 25 km from Utah Beach in a direct line, and more than twice that by road through the village of Isigny-sur-Mer on the River Vire, and the town of Carentan on the River Taute on the far side of the estuary mudflats.

In short, Omaha Beach was selected for the US V Corps landing because there was no other choice. It was critically important for troops from Omaha to get ashore rapidly on D-Day and to link up with the forces on either side. Failure at Omaha would leave the Allies with two beachheads, an Anglo-Canadian lodgement in front of Caen and an American lodgement in the Cotentin at Utah, too widely separated to help each other.

Physical communications east and west from Omaha depended on a narrow coastal road that ran along the

clifftop at variable distances up to about 1,200 metres from the edge. Small villages lay to either side of this clifftop road, of which the largest at Omaha were St-Laurent-sur-Mer in the centre and Colleville-sur-Mer to the east. (The French *sur mer* – 'on sea' – means in sight of the coast; there were other 'inland' Normandy villages with similar names.) Footpaths or tracks led off the beach up through each of the draws, the longest of which led back over 1,300 metres to Colleville. Two narrow paved roads led inland from the seafront at Vierville-sur-Mer at the western end of the beach and from St-Laurent, joining after about 3 km at the village of Formigny, just north of the only major road through the region (the modern N13). Known as the 'lateral road' in American planning, this ran through Caen and Bayeux, then on to Isigny and across the estuary to Carentan, and eventually north to Cherbourg.

The main objective for 21st Army Group was securing a landing deep enough to control the main Caen–Cherbourg lateral road along its length from Utah to Sword, with the added expectation that Second (British) Army would capture

There were several small towns in V Corps' assault area. This is the town centre of Isigny, 15 km south-west of Omaha Beach near the junction point with US VII Corps, which landed on Utah Beach. The buildings in the background can still be seen today. *(USNA)*

Maj Gen
Charles Corlett,
commander
of XIX Corps,
decorates
'Uncle Charlie'
Gerhardt,
commander of
29th Division,
later in the
Normandy battle.
(USNA)

Bayeux and Caen, and that patrols from all the beaches would reach deep inland. After D-Day, the plan was for Second (British) Army to advance well beyond Caen, threatening to break out towards Paris, while First US Army captured Cherbourg, securing the port as a supply base for the next phase of the campaign. The role of the troops coming ashore from Omaha was to form the bridge between these two forces, advancing inland after D-Day west of Bayeux and aiming to capture the town of St-Lô about 30 km south-west of Omaha Beach within a few days of landing.

For Operation Neptune responsibility for Utah and Omaha Beaches lay with Western Task Force (Task Force 122) under Rear Admiral Alan G. Kirk, US Navy. Part of this was Task Force O (for Omaha – or Task Force 124) commanded by Rear Admiral 'Jimmy' Hall, which sailed mainly from the ports of Weymouth, Portland and Poole on the south English coast, including a landing force of 34,142 men and 3,306 vehicles belonging to the reinforced 1st Infantry Division. Other troops of V Corps would arrive later on D-Day, transported by Follow-Up Force B (Task Force 126) under Commodore C.D. Edgar, altogether 25,117 men and 4,429 vehicles sailing from Plymouth, Falmouth and Fowey.

Commanded by Maj Gen Clarence R. Huebner, the veteran 1st Infantry Division (Motorized) was known as 'The Big Red One' from its famous shoulder patch of a large numeral '1' in red. For D-Day, Maj Gen Huebner would also command units of 29th Infantry Division under Maj Gen Charles ('Uncle Charlie') H. Gerhardt. Also taking part were two battalions of the elite US Rangers, each battalion comprising six small companies rather than the four larger companies of an infantry battalion. In a US Army that was largely a wartime creation, all these units took a pride in their history. Although formed in 1942,

ORDER OF BATTLE, OMAHA BEACH LANDING FORCES

V Corps — *Maj Gen Leonard T. Gerow*

Provisional Ranger Brigade Group — *Lt Col James E. Rudder*
Force A (D, E, F/2nd Rangers) — *Lt Col James E. Rudder*
Force B (C/2nd Rangers) — *Captain Ralph E. Goranson*
Force C (A & B/2nd R'gers A–F/5th R'gers) — *Lt Col Max F. Schneider*
Plus Cannon Company, 2 Naval Shore Fire Control Parties
1 Air Liaison Party

1st Infantry Division — *Maj Gen Clarence R. Huebner*
Assistant Commander — *Brig Gen Willard G. Wyman*
Artillery Commander — *Brig Gen C. Andrus*
16th Infantry Regiment — *Colonel George A. Taylor*
18th Infantry Regiment — *Colonel G. Smith*
26th Infantry Regiment — *Colonel J.F.R. Seitz*

5th Field Artillery Battalion; 7th Field Artillery Battalion;
32nd Field Artillery Battalion; 33rd Field Artillery Battalion;
1st Reconnaissance Troop; 1st Engineer Combat Battalion;
1st Medical Battalion; 1st Quartermaster Company; 1st Signal Company;
701st Ordnance Light Maintenance Company

Attached Units:
741st Tank Battalion; 745th Tank Battalion (from 3rd Armored Group);
20th Engineer Combat Battalion; part 81st Chemical Weapons Battalion;
62nd Armored Field Artillery Battalion; 635th Tank Destroyer Battalion
(from 3rd Armored Group, 7–11 June)

29th Infantry Division — *Maj Gen Charles H. Gerhardt*
Assistant Commander — *Brig Gen Norman D. Cota*
Artillery Commander — *Brig Gen William H. Sands*
115th Infantry Regiment* — *Colonel Eugene N. Slappey*
116th Infantry Regiment* — *Colonel Charles D. Canham*
175th Infantry Regiment — *Colonel Paul R. Goode*

110th Field Artillery Battalion; 111th Field Artillery Battalion;
224th Field Artillery Battalion; 227th Field Artillery Battalion;
29th Cavalry Reconnaissance Troop; 121st Engineer Combat Battalion;
104th Medical Battalion; 29th Quartermaster Company;
29th Signals Company; 729th Ordnance Light Maintenance Company

* These two regiments formed the Provisional Brigade attached to
1st Infantry Division on D-Day.

Attached Units:
743rd Tank Battalion; 747th Tank Battalion (from 3rd Armored Group,
7–13 June); 112th Engineer Combat Battalion; 102nd Cavalry
Reconnaissance Squadron; part 81st Chemical Weapons Battalion;
58th Armored Field Artillery Battalion; 635th Tank Destroyer Battalion
(from 3rd Armored Group)

Engineer Units
Detailed on page 69

Anti-Aircraft Artillery Units
Detailed on page 72

From left to right: Maj Gen Huebner (1st Infantry Division); Maj Gen Gerow (V Corps); and Brig Gen Hoge (Provisional Engineer Special Brigade Group). The photo was taken on board the USS *Ancon* on 5 June. *(US Naval Historical Center)*

the Rangers were named after Rogers' Rangers, a famed force of 18th century American frontiersmen. The Big Red One was the premier Regular Army division, and had already fought its way through North Africa, Sicily and Italy since 1942. The 29th Infantry Division was a National Guard division known as 'The Blue and Gray Division', originally recruited from states that had fought on the rival sides in the American Civil War. The division's 116th Infantry Regiment, which landed in the first wave together with 16th Infantry of 1st Infantry Division, was the 'Stonewall Brigade' from its origins as the 1st Virginia Brigade in the Civil War, commanded by the famous 'Stonewall' Jackson.

The beach at Omaha was wide enough for one division to land two regiments side by side; but V Corps needed to land two divisions on D-Day, one for each axis of advance, eastward towards Gold and westward towards Utah. The solution was to divide Omaha Beach in two just west of St-Laurent: 1st Infantry Division would land with a 'Provisional Brigade' of two infantry regiments under the assistant commander of 29th Infantry Division, Brigadier General (Brig Gen) Norman 'Dutch' Cota (who had previously served as chief of staff of 1st Infantry Division). Once enough troops were ashore, 29th Infantry Division headquarters would take over the western half of the advance inland.

The D-Day objectives for V Corps were for 1st Infantry Division to advance east almost to Port-en-Bessin and south-east to within 3 km of Bayeux to meet the British from Gold Beach. Meanwhile the regiments of 29th Infantry Division would advance westward on the coast road through Grandcamp and Maisy, and reach the Vire estuary, hopefully as far on as Isigny. Simultaneously, both divisions would also push southwards 2–3 km across the main Caen–Cherbourg lateral road, including securing the village of Trévières, directly south of Formigny.

These plans were drawn up to reflect the maximum that might be achieved on D-Day, but commanders knew that there would be both mistakes and surprises. As on the other D-Day beaches, the plans allowed 2–3 hours for the first troops to overcome the German defences and get tanks and other vehicles off the beach and inland. From the other perspective, a complete German success would be the defeat of the landings at the water's edge, and to drive V Corps back into the sea as Rommel intended.

CHAPTER 2

THE GERMAN DEFENCES

On 29 January 1944, visiting what would become Omaha Beach, an annoyed Rommel derided local commanders, 'You have been here three years and what have you achieved?' The Germans had used the seaside cottages, chalets and villas along the beach for bathing and recreation, and the *Hôtel du Casino* close to the beach at the bottom of the Vierville draw as a rest centre. The French civilian population stayed in their villages and chalets, and mostly continued their usual farming and fishing activities.

Rommel's appointment changed this as he demanded better defences for the Atlantic Wall. Local workmen were employed to cut tree-trunks from the extensive Cerisy forest, which lay inland astride the road from Bayeux to St-Lô, and cart these to the beach. Monsieur Michel Hardelay, the owner of a villa at Vierville, noted that from early 1944 onwards the Germans systematically demolished the chalets, using the wood and rubble to build their defences. By 6 June, out of 90 homes only seven remained, including Hardelay's own. The *Hôtel Degallois* next to the beach just downhill from the *Hôtel du Casino* was also demolished, and its foundations used as the base for a German bunker leaving the lower floor as camouflage, a trick repeated in other German defence works at Omaha.

The strength of these defences depended on the availability of labour and resources; there were numerous complaints about shortages of basic materials like concrete. The Allied air forces also repeatedly bombed targets on the Atlantic Wall to disrupt and slow construction, although for deception purposes they dropped twice as much tonnage outside the Normandy area as within it. Lower Normandy was itself a lesser priority for Rommel than the Pas de Calais, while if the Allies did choose Normandy the Germans expected them to land close to Cherbourg. A direct assault seemed unlikely, particularly after the disastrous failure in August 1942 of Operation 'Jubilee', the Allied attempt to capture the port of Dieppe in a surprise raid. More probably, the Germans believed, the Allies would land at the base of the Cotentin peninsula to take Cherbourg from the landward side, and their defensive scheme reflected this.

Both COSSAC and later SHAEF planners recognised the need to capture Cherbourg quickly after D-Day, but they had ruled out landing entirely in the Cotentin, chiefly because of the more rugged terrain, and because the Germans could seal up the peninsula after the first landings and trap the forces there. Until Cherbourg was captured the Allies planned to sustain their armies over the beaches by use of two prefabricated harbours towed across from England, code-named 'Mulberry'. One was to be built opposite St-Laurent on Omaha for First US Army, and the other at Arromanches for Second (British) Army. This was an innovation for which the Germans had not planned.

Until the Allies committed themselves to a landing, the commander of Seventh Army *Generaloberst* (Colonel-General) Friedrich Dollmann had to stretch his resources thinly across the whole of Lower Normandy and Brittany. The boundary between Fifteenth Army and Seventh Army

Opposite: The view from the lower slopes of WN-73, looking east along Omaha Beach at high tide. A German casemate, which contained a 50-mm anti-tank gun on 6 June, can be seen towards the upper right of the photo, with a large white door at its rear. Along with other positions this was part of WN-72, which helped defend the entrance to the Vierville draw. *(SCT)*

Generalleutnant Dietrich Kraiss, commander of the German 352nd Infantry Division, V Corps' principal opponent at the start of the Battle of Normandy. *(Bundesarchiv)*

lay just east of the River Orne. Within Seventh Army, Lower Normandy from the Orne to the western Cotentin came under LXXXIV Corps commanded by *General der Artillerie* (General of Artillery) Erich Marcks, with his headquarters at St-Lô. This was a considerable area to defend, within which General Marcks's priority was Cherbourg rather than the Calvados coast.

A visible consequence of Hitler's directive giving priority to the west was the arrival of veterans from the Eastern Front (*Ostkämpfer* or 'East-fighters'), bringing with them many lessons particularly about defence. By this stage of the war, the German Army in the west (*Westheer*) was being forced to improvise in many ways. There were expedients and variations in the size and structure of units, and captured weapons, particularly from France and Czechoslovakia, were pressed into service. The Atlantic Wall defences followed a standard general pattern, but also with many local variations and improvisations. German record-keeping was often meticulous, but some records were lost or contained errors, and later veterans' recollections differed from each other. The Allies also analysed the German defences of Normandy before D-Day, and produced reports after the battle. Although differences exist in these various sources, the shape of the German defences at Omaha Beach can still be accurately described.

The division originally assigned to defend the Calvados coastline from Caen to Carentan, known as 'Coast Defence Sector H', was 716th Infantry Division under *Generalleutnant* (GenLt) Wilhelm Richter. This formation was typical of the 'static' (*Bodenständige*) infantry divisions that the *Westheer* created to carry out defensive tasks, partly made up of over-aged men, strong in artillery, but with little or no transport. Among its infantry regiments was 726th Grenadiers of three battalions. Attached to this regiment was 439th Ost Battalion, one of the division's three *Ost-Bataillone* ('East-Battalions'), recruited in eastern Europe from a mixture of prisoners of war and some volunteers, and described as 'Russian'. In November 1943, the new 352nd Infantry Division began to form at St-Lô, commanded by GenLt Dietrich Kraiss (written as Kraiß in German) and composed partly of veterans from two divisions that had served on the Eastern Front. This was a higher quality formation with three infantry regiments each of two battalions, an artillery regiment with 36 towed 105-mm guns and 12 150-mm howitzers, and an anti-tank battalion including 10 Sturmgeschütze III and 14 Marder III tracked assault guns. By April 1944 the division had its full complement of weapons and troops, at least 13,228 men, including Poles, Ukrainians, Georgians and even Mongolians as well as Germans. Allied intelligence (and several senior German commanders), believed both before and after D-Day that these *Ost* soldiers would not fight for Germany. But although they were seldom loyal to the Nazi cause, and were prepared to surrender in the right circumstances, they surprised Seventh Army headquarters with their fighting qualities. Training was limited because of the need to build the Atlantic Wall, although part of the division's work was done by 1,500 *Hiwis* (a uniformed corps of eastern labourers, from *Hilfswillige*, 'a voluntary aide'). Unlike many German units that fought in Normandy, 352nd Infantry Division was rated fit for active service on the Eastern Front, the standard benchmark for a strong and well-trained division.

Due to Rommel's demands for defence at the water's edge, in March 1944 352nd Infantry Division was ordered to take over part of the Calvados coastline. In the new arrangement, 716th Infantry Division retained responsibility for 'Coast Defence Sector Caen' stretching from Asnelles east to the Orne, where the British would land on D-Day, while 352nd Infantry Division took the newly-created 'Coast Defence Sector Bayeux' (also documented as 'Coast Defence Sector H2'), from Carentan

GERMAN DEFENCES ON OMAHA BEACH

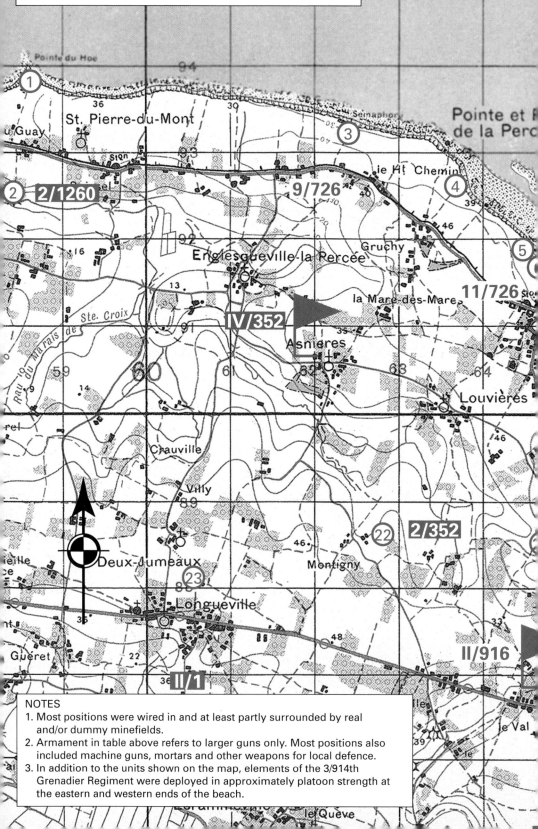

NOTES

1. Most positions were wired in and at least partly surrounded by real and/or dummy minefields.
2. Armament in table above refers to larger guns only. Most positions also included machine guns, mortars and other weapons for local defence.
3. In addition to the units shown on the map, elements of the 3/914th Grenadier Regiment were deployed in approximately platoon strength at the eastern and western ends of the beach.

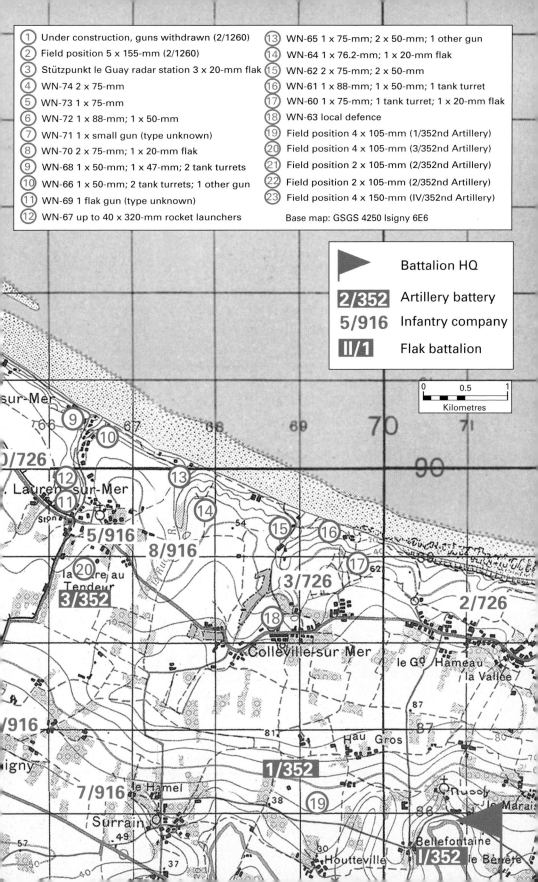

1. Under construction, guns withdrawn (2/1260)
2. Field position 5 x 155-mm (2/1260)
3. Stützpunkt le Guay radar station 3 x 20-mm flak
4. WN-74 2 x 75-mm
5. WN-73 1 x 75-mm
6. WN-72 1 x 88-mm; 1 x 50-mm
7. WN-71 1 x small gun (type unknown)
8. WN-70 2 x 75-mm; 1 x 20-mm flak
9. WN-68 1 x 50-mm; 1 x 47-mm; 2 tank turrets
10. WN-66 1 x 50-mm; 2 tank turrets; 1 other gun
11. WN-69 1 flak gun (type unknown)
12. WN-67 up to 40 x 320-mm rocket launchers
13. WN-65 1 x 75-mm; 2 x 50-mm; 1 other gun
14. WN-64 1 x 76.2-mm; 1 x 20-mm flak
15. WN-62 2 x 75-mm; 2 x 50-mm
16. WN-61 1 x 88-mm; 1 x 50-mm; 1 tank turret
17. WN-60 1 x 75-mm; 1 tank turret; 1 x 20-mm flak
18. WN-63 local defence
19. Field position 4 x 105-mm (1/352nd Artillery)
20. Field position 4 x 105-mm (3/352nd Artillery)
21. Field position 2 x 105-mm (2/352nd Artillery)
22. Field position 2 x 105-mm (2/352nd Artillery)
23. Field position 4 x 150-mm (IV/352nd Artillery)

Base map: GSGS 4250 Isigny 6E6

Battalion HQ

2/352 Artillery battery

5/916 Infantry company

II/1 Flak battalion

0   0.5   1
Kilometres

east to Asnelles. As part of this change, 352nd Infantry Division took under its command 726th Grenadiers with two of its battalions and 439th *Ost* Battalion, along with other troops formerly of 716th Infantry Division.

Now with four infantry regiments, GenLt Kraiss divided his frontage into three sectors, rotating his regiments between them and a reserve held just inland. On D-Day, 'Coast Defence Sector 1' from Carentan to Grandcamp was defended by 914th Grenadier Regiment with its headquarters near Isigny, supported by 2nd Battalion, 352nd Artillery Regiment, (II/352nd Artillery) with 439th Ost Battalion nearby and most of the assault guns of 352nd Anti-tank Battalion just further south. 'Coast Defence Sector 2' from Grandcamp to Colleville-sur-Mer, including most of Omaha Beach, was defended by 916th Grenadier Regiment, incorporating 3rd Battalion, 726th Grenadier Regiment (III/726th Grenadiers) with its headquarters near Grandcamp and its companies spread as far east as Vierville, and II/916th Grenadiers with two companies forward defending the central part of Omaha Beach, and another two companies in reserve near Formigny. Shortly before D-Day, most of 3rd Company 914th Grenadiers was sent to reinforce Omaha Beach, being divided between WN-73 and the eastern end of the beach. Their artillery support was 12 105-mm howitzers of I/352nd Artillery and four 150-mm howitzers that were part of IV/352nd Artillery. From Colleville-sur-Mer to Asnelles, 'Coast Defence Sector 3' was the responsibility of 726th Grenadiers (I/726th and I/916th) with III/352nd Artillery in support. The local reserve for LXXXIV Corps, *Kampfgruppe* (Battle Group) Meyer was located south and east of Bayeux, comprising the two battalions of 915th Grenadiers (Kraiss' fourth regiment) under *Oberstleutnant* (Lieutenant Colonel – Lt Col) Karl Meyer, together with 352nd Fusilier Battalion. Battle Group *Meyer* was equipped with bicycles except for I/915th Grenadiers which was motorised in French civilian trucks.

The transfer of units from 716th Infantry Division to 352nd Infantry Division without their changing location may have contributed to a rare failure of Allied intelligence, which

had a reasonably good record of identifying German units in Normandy before the battle. Late detection of an unexpected German division, 91st Airlanding Division, in the Cotentin led to changes in the airborne plan for Utah Beach on 27 May that saved many American lives. But Allied estimates continued to show 352nd Infantry Division as deployed inland near St-Lô. The intelligence failure was so unexpected that after D-Day a story spread rapidly, and was believed for many years, that 352nd Infantry Division had only moved up from St-Lô a few days before D-Day to conduct an anti-invasion training exercise, and that its presence at Omaha was unforeseeable bad luck.

On the morning of D-Day, First US Army's assessment was that no more than a reinforced battalion of 800–1,000 men from 716th Infantry Division defended Omaha, with perhaps another two battalions able to reach the area within 2–3 hours; further, that it would be late afternoon before 352nd Infantry Division from St-Lô could get even a regiment to Omaha, and that no other reserve forces would intervene. It was also not expected that 716th Infantry

GERMAN ORDER OF BATTLE

LXXXIV CORPS   *General der Artillerie Erich Marcks*

352nd Infantry Division *(352. Infanterie-Division)*

Generalleutnant Dietrich Kraiss

914th Grenadier Regiment	*Oberstleutnant Ernst Heyna*
915th Grenadier Regiment	*Oberstleutnant Karl Meyer*
916th Grenadier Regiment	*Oberst Ernst Goth*
726th Grenadier Regiment*	*Oberst Walter Korfes*
352nd Artillery Regiment	*Oberstleutnant Karl-Wilhelm Ocker*
352nd Anti-tank Battalion	*Hauptmann Jahn*
352nd Fusilier Battalion	*Hauptmann Gerth*
352nd Engineer Battalion	

* attached from 716th Infantry Division

1st Anti-Aircraft Assault Regiment *(Flak-Sturm-Regiment 1)*

Oberst Paul von Kistowski

30th Mobile Brigade *(Schnelle Brigade 30)*

Oberstleutnant Freiherr von Aufsess

84th Rocket Launcher Regiment *(Werfer-Regiment 84)* (elements)

This extract from the 1:25000 scale map issued to US troops shortly before the invasion shows the coastline west of Omaha Beach. The amendments to the map (in red) reflected the latest information available to Allied intelligence. Notable features include the radar station near the Pointe et Raz de la Percée and the gun position at the Pointe du Hoc (mislabelled as 'Hoe').
Base map: GSGS 4347 St. Pierre-du-Mont 34/18NE, Stop Press edition, 20 May 1944.

Division would fight well. The Allies believed that static divisions were of poor quality, neglecting the fact that they were structured to be strong in defence. Certainly, American propaganda photographs taken after D-Day showed baby-faced youths and grey-haired old men among their prisoners, but many soldiers of 726th Grenadiers fought hard.

The basis of the German defences was a chain of coastal gun batteries supporting emplacements, bunkers and trench systems with heavy weapons and machine guns defending the beaches. The most common of the bunker complexes were 'resistance nests' (*Widerstandsnester*), designated as WN-1, WN-2, etc. These varied in size and design but typically held 30–50 men as gun crews and infantry in a mixture of concrete emplacements and earth entrenchments, protected by wire and mines. Despite Rommel's strategy, the experience of the *Ostkämpfer* also led to 352nd Infantry Division holding reserves deeper inland.

The coastal batteries in LXXXIV Corps' area were positioned chiefly to defend either Cherbourg or Le Havre, and because of its central position there were only two heavy batteries covering the sea approaches to Omaha Beach. On the clifftops at Longues-sur-Mer, 11 km east of Omaha in the heart of Le Chaos, was a Navy battery (*Marine-Küsten-Batterie*), with four 150-mm guns taken from a decommissioned warship and fixed into casemates, with a garrison of about 150 sailors averaging 40–45 years old, taken under Army command as 4th Battery of the 1260th Army Coastal Artillery Battalion (4/1260th Coastal Artillery or 4/1260 HKAA). The other casemated battery, with six French 155-mm guns on wheeled carriages, was built on the clifftop heights of the Pointe du Hoc, 12 km to the west of Omaha. Originally this was 2/832nd Coastal Artillery Battalion (2/HKAA 832), officially known as the Criqueville-en-Bessin battery from the village immediately inland. In December 1943 as part of the strengthening of the Atlantic Wall it was renumbered 2/1260th Coastal Artillery (2/HKAA 1260), and work commenced building new and stronger casemates and upgrading the surrounding defences to the status of a 'strongpoint' (*Stützpunkt*)

A French 155-mm howitzer (designated by the Germans as the 15.5 cm K420[f]) in an open emplacement at the Pointe du Hoc. This position was successfully attacked by US Rangers on D-Day. The guns themselves were discovered (and destroyed) a kilometre or so inland, having been moved there in an attempt to protect them against air attack. (Bundesarchiv)

manned by 125 men of III/726th Grenadiers as *Stützpunkt Bayeux* 075 (S-75). Like many German mobile batteries along the Atlantic Wall, the guns had alternative firing positions made of earth and timber, and they were withdrawn a short distance while the new casemates were built, work delayed by Allied bombing and by higher priorities elsewhere, and incomplete on 6 June.

Evidence is disputed about the exact location of the Pointe du Hoc guns on D-Day, but regardless of this the battery constituted the biggest threat to the ships of Task Force O. Both the Pointe du Hoc and Longues positions were heavily bombed by the RAF from April onwards, Longues twice, on 28 May and 3 June, and Pointe du Hoc at least five times, the last on 5 June. Because the Longues battery lay on the eastern side of the 21st Army Group boundary, sited predominantly to fire on the approaches to Gold Beach, it was a British responsibility for D-Day. The Pointe du Hoc battery was made a special target in V Corps' plans: three companies of 2nd Rangers under Lt Col James E. Rudder would go in with the first landing wave and attack the battery by scaling the sheer 30-metre cliff-face, with the remaining Rangers arriving later as reinforcements.

No other heavy casemated guns threatened the approach to Omaha, which in this respect was lightly defended compared to the other D-Day beaches, but German defences dominated the cliffs on either side. High on the

Pointe et Raz de la Percée was *Stützpunkt le Guay* with troops of III/726th Grenadiers defending a Navy radar station with two 'Giant Würzburg' and one 'Freya' radar. Part of the furthest western D-Day objectives for V Corps at Maisy and nearby Géfosse was a complex of strongpoints and resistance nests including two batteries originally from 716th Infantry Division: 9/1716th Artillery with four 100-mm Czech guns and 8/1716th Artillery. Before D-Day Allied intelligence believed both batteries to be heavy. The guns lacked the range to fire on the approaches to Omaha, but like those at the Pointe du Hoc they could be moved, and they threatened the advance of 29th Infantry Division westward. They could also fire across the Vire estuary onto Utah Beach.

For planning purposes, the Allies subdivided each of their landing beaches into segments given their own code-names. Out to sea from Omaha Beach was Area Elder, including the Transport Area for the landing ships and craft of Task Force O to assemble before the landings began. From the Line of Departure for the assault, 4,000 metres offshore, the sea was divided into Area Oregon, the landing area west of St-Laurent for the troops of 29th Infantry Division, and Area Ohio for the troops of 1st Infantry Division. Omaha Beach itself was divided, like all the Allied landing beaches, into segments (technically 'beach landing areas') using the military phonetic alphabet, and further subdivided by colours. To the west, 29th Infantry

US A-20 Havocs bomb the Pointe du Hoc battery on 25 April 1944. One of the battery's six guns may have been destroyed in this raid. *(USNA)*

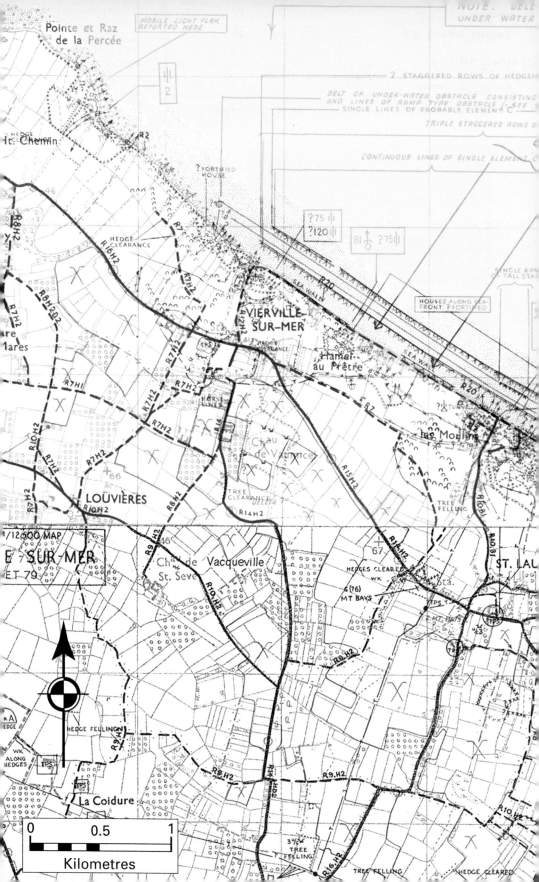

This detailed 1:25000 scale map shows the German defences at Omaha Beach, as appreciated by Allied intelligence on 20 May 1944. As well as a considerable thickening of beach obstacles (like other recent intelligence, marked in red), it shows evidence of German attempts to erect clusters of anti-glider landing poles inland; these are indicated by large red diagonal crosses. Barbed wire fences are shown as strings of small 'x's, while minefields (real or dummy) are indicated by inverted horseshoe symbols. The lack of beach obstacles in Easy sector is clearly shown. The dense nature of the *bocage*, punctuated by numerous orchards (e.g. at Colleville-sur-Mer), is also immediately apparent. *Base maps: GSGS 4347 St. Pierre-du-Mont 34/18NE, Trévières 34/18SE and Ryes 37/18SW, Stop Press edition, 20 May 1944.*

A typical German obstacle on Omaha Beach, constructed from a tree trunk driven into the sand and braced with a steel frame. The obstacle is topped by an anti-tank mine, which was designed to blast holes in landing craft running over the top of it at high tide. (*IWM AP23388*)

Division planned to land on Dog Green, Dog White, and Dog Red beaches and on Easy Green beach. Its landing objectives were the draw inland at Vierville on Dog Green code-named Dog-1, and another leading inland to St-Laurent at the little beachside hamlet of les Moulins ('The Windmills') on Dog Red code-named Dog-3. The troops of 1st Infantry Division planned to land on Easy Red Beach and Fox Green Beach, and their objectives were the draws at Easy-1, the Ruquet valley between St-Laurent and Colleville on Easy Red Beach, and Easy-3 on the boundary between Easy Red and Fox Green Beaches, leading to Colleville itself. Just to the east on Fox Red beach was a fifth and smaller valley called 'la Révolution', shallow and steep with only a rough trail, code-named Fox-1, east of which were the cliffs.

Two necessities for the Allied landings were broad and gently shelving beaches suitable for heavy vehicles, and reasonable ground inland for their advance. At Omaha Beach, the ten fathom line (18 metres), considered the safe limit of deep water for the bombarding warships of Task Force O (Bombarding Force C), was roughly 5 km from the shore. Low tide at Omaha on D-Day was 0530 hours, shortly before dawn at 0556, exposing 330 metres of firm sand, shelving inland at a virtually imperceptible gradient of no more than 1:190. This gradient increased to 1:47 at the top of the beach, where there was normally up to 150 metres of exposed dry sand at high tide some six hours later. At 0630 hours, at least 300 metres of tidal beach was still exposed and the water in which the first American landing craft touched down averaged barely 50 cm deep, or roughly knee high. But at Omaha, more than any of the other landing beaches, the shape of the bay produced strong west-to- east currents of at least 5 km/hr (2.7 knots). Among other hazards the scouring effect dug runnels in the sand, creating sandbars alternating with pockets sometimes over 150 cm deep, an unexpected trap for a wading man carrying heavy equipment who could suddenly be plunged neck-deep in water.

The Germans expected the Allies to land close to high tide, and the tidal beach at Omaha was covered with obstacles meant to be submerged beneath the water at that time. The scouring currents and twice daily tides meant that these obstacles needed constant repair, and made it impractical to lay land mines in the sand. Instead, anti-tank mines (*Tellerminen*) were fitted directly onto the obstacles. About 250 metres from high water was a broken line of 'Belgian gates' or 'Type C' obstacles, each resembling a farm gate made of metal girders about three metres square built onto a railway buffer, facing out to sea. Allied reports counted 200 of these, with a small gap in the middle of Dog White beach, and a much larger gap across the whole 1,800-metre frontage of Easy Red beach, possibly as a deliberate trap. The remaining lines of obstacles were all continuous. Arranged in successive rows 30 metres up the beach were 2,000 *Holzpfäle*, thick wooden stakes or posts erected by driving tree trunks into the sand, 2–3 metres high and angled away from the shore, about every third post topped with an anti-tank mine. A further 30 metres up the beach was another line of 450 shallow ramps (*Hemmbalken*) 3–4 metres long sloping up towards the shore and supported by a bipod, most made from segments of tree-trunk and the remainder from curved metal rails, also fitted with mines. The intention was for flat-bottomed landing craft to ride up these ramps as they came inshore, and either explode or flip over. Finally, half-way up the landing beach, 150 metres from high water, was a line of 1,050 metal caltrops or 'Czech hedgehogs' (*Tschechenigel*) made by welding three girders each 2–3 metres in length together, and a few solid concrete pyramids of the same height.

The beach defences at Omaha were substantial, and in a good state of repair, a major problem for vehicles and for landing craft delivering troops as the incoming tide covered them in the course of the morning. Part of V Corps' plan was that specialist engineers would land with the first wave, led by 16 Gap Assault Teams each of 33 soldiers and sailors of the Special Engineer Task Force supported by an armoured 'tankdozer'. Their task was to clear gaps through the German obstacles.

At the top of the tidal beach at Omaha was a considerable natural obstacle for vehicles: an uneven bank of pebbles, small rocks and shingle about 15 metres wide and almost 3 metres high in places. This was fronted on the western part of the beach by a concrete seawall carrying a beachfront road from Dog-1 draw at Vierville to Dog-3 at les Moulins, faced by wooden palings for part of its length. The road and the beach to the east beyond les Moulins were backed by a deep anti-tank ditch and covered by a thick belt of concertina barbed wire. Beyond this, leading to the bluffs, was a plain composed of sand alternating with marsh (produced by the Germans damming up small streams) and with solid earth covered with undergrowth on which most of the seaside chalets had been built, varying from 100 metres wide at its western end to 300 metres wide in the centre at Dog-3 and Easy-1. Barbed wire, minefields, and anti-tank ditches covered the gaps between the resistance nests, and the roads and tracks inland were also mined for about 500 metres.

The Omaha bluffs themselves were steeper towards the western end of the beach, covered with grass and undergrowth, but unlike the cliffs they were not sheer, and a footsoldier could pick his way up rather than climbing. Dug into the heights of the bluffs, or at their foot for low-trajectory grazing fire, were 15 resistance nests numbered from WN-60 in the east, at the Fox-1 la Révolution valley, to WN-73 and WN-74 at the start of the cliffs west of Vierville, with the heights of the bluffs between them defended by wire and land mines. These defences, connected by trenches along the top of the bluffs and by underground

The anti-tank ditch near the Easy-1 draw, looking east. The ditch was 4½ metres deep and ran parallel with the beach, 140 metres from the high water mark. There were anti-tank ditches on both sides of the Easy-1 draw, as well as at les Moulins (Dog-3) and in front of the Colleville exit (Easy-3). *(IWM PL26754)*

tunnels, were manned by five companies of infantry: 10/726th and 11/726th Grenadiers to the west, then 5/916th and 8/916th Grenadiers, and 3/726th Grenadiers.

Most of the resistance nests were built in pairs on opposite sides of a draw to provide mutually-supporting crossfire, sited to fire along the beach rather than directly out to sea. Some had only machine guns and mortars, but most had heavier weapons including anti-tank guns and automatic flame-throwers, and firing points made by fitting a captured French tank turret onto a concrete ring. The largest at Omaha was WN-62 guarding the western side of Easy-3, a substantial complex of bunkers and trenches over 1,300 metres in circumference built into the forward slope of the bluff from the 50 metre contour almost to sea level, and surrounded by barbed wire. Its defences included two Czech 75-mm guns and a 50-mm anti-tank gun, mortars, machine guns, and forward spotters for the field guns of I/352nd Artillery.

On the eastern side of the Easy-3 draw, WN-61 was built into the base of the bluff with an 88-mm dual-purpose anti-aircraft/anti-tank gun, the most feared artillery piece in the German armoury, capable of destroying Allied tanks at ranges of up to 2,500 metres. This gun was positioned to interlock its long-range fire with a matching 88-mm gun located 5 km to the west at WN-72, built onto the remains of the *Hôtel Degallois* on the beachfront at the bottom of Dog-1. Itself the strongest position on the beach, WN-72 was part of a complex of four resistance nests defending Dog-1 and Vierville. Together, the *Widerstandsnester* on Omaha Beach were equipped with at least 18 anti-tank guns, 85 machine guns, 15 mortars, nine tank turrets and three field guns.

In combination with the beach obstacles, the mines and wire, and the bluffs themselves, this made Omaha the most heavily defended of all the D-Day beaches. But there were some weaknesses. After-battle analysis found that only 15 per cent of 352nd Infantry Division's positions were bomb-proof, and 45 per cent were proof against shell splinters. Not all of the resistance nests on Omaha were completed on D-Day, including WN-65 defending Easy-1 draw, and some lacked weapons for their emplacements. At the far eastern end of the beach below WN-60 there was dead ground at the foot of the cliffs, where German fire could not reach. There was also a much longer 750-metre stretch of dead ground, covered only by mines and wire, at the foot of the bluff on Easy Red between WN-62 and WN-64, opposite part of the gap in the Belgian gates. Despite their nomenclature the three *Widerstandsnester* at the top of the bluffs along the coast road did not represent a second line of defence. WN-63 immediately north-east of Colleville village was the company command post for 3/726th Grenadiers,

The Germans attempted to close several of the draws along Omaha Beach (and elsewhere) by constructing substantial concrete and masonry walls to block the passage of vehicles inland. Here two American soldiers pick their way across the rubble from one such wall in the devastated village of les Moulins. *(IWM PL26096)*

with no heavy weapons. Near St-Laurent, WN-69 was incomplete with no concrete structures; and WN-67 nearby on the nose of high ground at the top of Dog-3 draw was the location for elements of 84th Rocket Launcher Regiment with an estimated 20–40 'rocket pits' each fitted to fire four *Nebelwerfer*-type 320-mm rockets, known as 'Screaming Meemies' or 'Moaning Minnies' by Allied troops. It is unclear whether or not this last position was occupied on D-Day.

Those American troops who reached the top of the bluffs were at once confronted with what Lt Gen Bradley called 'the damnedest country I've seen', the Normandy hedgerow country or *bocage*. The coastal road and the road inland to Formigny were bounded on either side by trees and by stone walls or thick hedgerows. The same pattern of trees and hedgerows obscured the shape of a substantial ridge running parallel to the coast, 2–4 km across and rising to nearly 80 metres before falling away into the valley of the River Aure (known for this stretch as the Lower Aure or l'Aure Inférieure). Barely more than a stream, the Aure flowed northwards through Bayeux before turning sharply westward, crossing under the main Caen–Cherbourg road 4 km directly south of Omaha, and flowing into the River Vire at Isigny. West of Omaha the Germans had blocked the Aure to produce flooding and an extended marsh, making the north side of this river valley a natural part of the planned American halt-line for D-Day.

The defences at Omaha Beach included two 88-mm anti-tank guns. This is the 88-mm gun casemate at WN-72, defending the entrance to the Dog-1 draw near Vierville. Like the similar position at WN-61, 5 km further east, the gun was sited to enfilade the beach, rather than shoot out to sea. The concrete wall provided protection against fire from the seaward side and hid the gun's muzzle flash, making it difficult to locate. *(USNA)*

Bocage country. Thick field hedges like these characterised most of the hinterland of Omaha Beach. This photo shows the track leading from the coastal road (now the D514) to the positions held by the forward elements of the US 2nd Rangers on the evening of 6 June near the Pointe du Hoc. (TB)

The *bocage* country itself was the product of farming practices centuries old, with small irregular fields and dairy pastures marked by stone walls or by deeply-rooted hedgerows, often growing into raised earth banks. In the open fields, the Germans had driven wooden poles or tree trunks 2–3 metres high, known as 'Rommel's Asparagus' (*Rommelsspargel*), into the ground as a defence against glider landings. Narrow lanes or dirt tracks overgrown with trees and bounded by stone or earth ran through gullies between the fields; the road inland to Formigny resembled a twisting tunnel, and the village itself lay in a hollow. The villages, farmhouses, and country houses like the Château du Vaumicel (just inland from Vierville) were thick stone constructions with deep cellars almost like fortresses. In June with the apple trees in leaf and the crops growing, the hedgerows were blind country, a defender's paradise in which locating targets for artillery and naval gunfire was difficult, and even tanks moved in constant fear of ambush.

On this ridge the Germans placed their second line of defence, dug into the hedgerows or barricaded in the houses and barns. Headquarters for II/916th Grenadiers was at Formigny, with its two reserve companies spread out from the main Caen–Cherbourg road northwards to the top of the bluff: 7/916th Grenadiers at Surrain with 6/916th Grenadiers to its west. Three 105-mm batteries of I/352nd Artillery were dug into the fields in a line 10 km westwards from

its headquarters at Étréham: 1/352nd Artillery to the east, 3/105th Artillery in the centre just north of Formigny, and 2/352nd Artillery in two positions to the west, plus the four 150-mm guns from IV/352nd Artillery; all were linked by buried telephone cables with the spotters in WN-62 above Easy-3 draw waiting to bring down fire onto Omaha Beach.

Further inland, beyond the Caen–Cherbourg lateral road and the Lower Aure, was a weaker third line of defence. At Trévières was 916th Grenadiers' regimental HQ, and 3 km to the east and west were 2nd and 3rd Battalions, 1st Anti-Aircraft Assault Regiment (*Flak-Sturm-Regiment 1*), with 1st Battalion further south-west at Mestry on the far side of the flooded river valley. This regiment was detached from III Flak Corps, a *Luftwaffe* formation otherwise assigned to Fifteenth Army, and was meant for anti-aircraft defence of the Bayeux area. Each battalion had at least twelve 88-mm guns, sited well within range of the lateral road about 1,500 metres away, but because of German command arrangements, the Army had no control over 1st AA Assault Regiment on D-Day. Further to the south, close to Cerisy forest, were 352nd Engineer Battalion and at least some of the 14 Marder assault guns of 352nd Anti-Tank Battalion. Except for what they could learn from air reconnaissance and other sources, these defences were unknown to the Allies.

US Army ordnance personnel examine three remote-controlled 'Goliath' demolition vehicles near Omaha Beach. Goliaths were deployed along the Lower Normandy coast, but there is no evidence of them being used effectively on D-Day. *(USNA)*

CHAPTER 3

THE D-DAY LANDINGS

US vessels of Force O-1's LCI(L) Coast Guard Flotilla 10 await the order to sail shortly before D-Day. *LCI(L) 85*, at left, was sunk on D-Day. *(USNA)*

In the first days of June bad weather swept through the English Channel, with low cloud, heavy rain, and high winds. The assault troops had all been embarked when, at 0415 hours on 4 June, Eisenhower's HQ at Southwick House near Portsmouth ordered the postponement of D-Day for 24 hours. Some ships had already set sail for their objectives and had to be recalled or pause at sea. These included several ships of Force O, the battleship USS *Texas* from Belfast, and slow convoy B-1 from Plymouth, one of the three convoys (B-1, B-2 and B-3) of Follow-Up Force B.

At 2130 hours on 4 June, with the support of his assembled commanders, Eisenhower decided on 6 June

as D-Day. The weather was improving, but still marginal; 'I don't like it, but there it is,' Eisenhower said, 'I don't see how we can do anything else'. Unknown to the Allies, Rommel had left his own HQ at la Roche-Guyon château, 40 km northwest of Paris, on 4 June to visit his family home in Bavaria prior to a planned meeting with Hitler. Driving flat-out on hearing of the invasion on 6 June, he would not get back to la Roche-Guyon until 1700 hours.

The ships and larger landing craft of Task Force O started to steam for Omaha at 1600 hours on 5 June, forming up into convoys and heading into the English Channel. Through the night, the wider plans for Operation Neptune began to shape the battle for Omaha Beach next morning. RAF and USAAF bombing of the landing areas began at about 2230 hours, with B-24 Liberator heavy bombers of USAAF Eighth Air Force's 2nd Bombardment Division hitting 13 targets between Port-en-Bessin and the Pointe et Raz de la Percée. French Resistance fighters and Allied specialists began sabotage and deception measures across Normandy. Soon after 2300 hours Seventh Army went on alert in response to suspicions regarding coded radio messages for the Resistance sent through the BBC. From just after midnight, British gliders and paratroopers began to land east of the River Orne, and American paratroopers in the Cotentin inland from Utah Beach, close to the small town of Ste-Mère-Eglise on the main Cherbourg road. Thick low cloud interfered with the American drop, and many of the paratroopers were scattered far from their targets, some landing close to Carentan. At least two planeloads were dropped well to the east

Rear Admiral John Hall, commander of Task Force O, photographed on his flagship, the USS *Ancon*. (USNA)

US soldiers use scramble nets to board their transport ship from LCVPs in a British harbour. In heavy seas, with troops who were cold, wet and afraid, the task of reversing the process could be a difficult and time-consuming one. *(USNA)*

beyond Grandcamp and there is an unconfirmed story of paratroopers attacking a German position at Omaha Beach that night; at least one paratrooper definitely fought at the Pointe du Hoc next morning.

One important result of the Allied airborne landings was to suck in the German local reserves, leaving them unavailable to defend against the daylight beach landings. At 0145 hours, in response to reports of landings in the Vire estuary (six planeloads dropped far from their targets), two companies of II/914th Grenadiers near Isigny moved out into the night to hunt them down. At 0322 hours, IV/352nd Artillery reported that its positions were being heavily bombed, and in response 352nd Infantry Division increased its alert status. Bombing intensified after 0335 hours as 1,327 RAF Bomber Command aircraft hit targets, among them the Pointe du Hoc battery, across Lower Normandy. True to its own preconceptions of the battle, Seventh Army identified the point of main effort (*Schwerpunkt* in German) of the Allied

landings as Ste-Mère-Eglise, with the object of cutting off the Cotentin at its base, and planned a counter-attack. By 0420 hours LXXXIV Corps' reserve, 352nd Infantry Division's Battle Group Meyer, was on its way west from Bayeux to a position south of Carentan as a precaution. The direct threat from paratroopers to Carentan failed to materialise, and just as dawn was breaking *Meyer*'s force, which had already bicycled and driven to west of Cerisy forest, was ordered to halt.

To allow time for an effective shore bombardment, and to ensure that deeper water covered the shoals offshore from their beaches, the British planned to start their landings at 0725–0735 hours. Western Task Force and First US Army decided to commence an hour earlier than the British, giving barely more than 30 minutes of daylight before the first landings, and to launch their landing craft from over 17,600 metres (11 miles) offshore to be out of range of German coastal batteries. This meant the ships and craft taking station in the dark, and a sick-making journey (planned at Omaha to start at 0455 hours) for the men in the flat-bottomed landing craft ploughing southwards into the strong cross-current and prevailing westerly wind. The weather remained poor, with a partial overcast and intermittent rain, winds of 18–34 km/hr (10–18 knots), and a sea-swell 1–2 metres high. At Utah, although the wind and current pushed the first landing craft some 2 km further south than was planned, the landing took place very successfully. But at Omaha nothing was going to go right.

Ships of Bombarding Force C on 5 June. In the lead is the battleship USS *Texas*, followed by the cruiser HMS *Glasgow*, the battleship USS *Arkansas* and the two French cruisers *Georges Leygues* and (just visible) *Montcalm*. All played an important role in supporting V Corps' assault the following day. (IWM A23923)

ALLIED NAVAL FORCES AT OMAHA BEACH
6 June 1944

TASK FORCE 122: WESTERN TASK FORCE
Rear Admiral Alan G. Kirk, USN [USS *Augusta*]
Lieutenant General Omar N. Bradley *First US Army*

Task Force 124: Task Force O
Rear Admiral John L. Hall Jr. [ACG 4 USS *Ancon*]
Major General Leonard T. Gerow V Corps

Assault Group O1: Easy Red Beach – Fox Green Beach
Captain E.H. Fritzsche, USCG [APA 26 USS *Samuel Chase*]
Deputy: *Captain M.H. Imlay, USCG* [*LCH 87*]

APA/LSI(L) Unit
APA 26 USS *Samuel Chase*	(1/16th RCT)
APA 45 USS *Henrico*	(2/16th RCT)
LSI(L) SS *Empire Anvil*	(3/16th RCT)

LST Unit
LST 309, LST 314, LST 357, LST 373, LST 374, LST 376

LCC 10, LCC 20

LCI(L) 5 craft; LCT 53 craft; LCM 18 craft

Assault Group O2: Dog Beach – Easy Green Beach

Captain W.O. Bailey, USN [APA 28 USS *Charles Carroll*]
Deputy: *Captain W. D. Wright, USN* [*LCH 86*]

APA/LSI(L) Unit
APA 28 USS *Charles Carroll*	(3/116th RCT)
APA 30 USS *Thomas Jefferson*	(2/116th RCT)
LSI(L) SS *Empire Javelin*	(1/116th RCT)

LST Unit
LST 310, LST 315, LST 316, LST 317, LST 332, LST 372

LCC 30; LCC 40; LCC 50

LCI(L) 17 craft; LCT 54 craft; LCM 18 craft

Assault Group O3: Easy Red Beach, Fox Green Beach

Captain L.B. Schulten, USN [AP 76 USS *Anne Arundel*]
Deputy: *Commander A.C. Unger, USCG* [*LCH 492*]

AP Unit
AP 76 USS *Anne Arundel*	(2/18th Infantry Regt)
AP 67 USS *Dorothea L. Dix*	(various units)
AP 77 USS *Thurston*	(various units)

LST Unit
LST 6, LST 51, LST 75, LST 133, LST 134, LST 157, LST 285, LST 286, LST 347, LST 350, LST 375, LST 502.

LCI(L) 11 craft; LCT 39 craft; LSD HMS *Oceanway*

Assault Group O4: Pointe du Hoc and Dog Green Beach
Commander S.H. Dennis, RN [LSI(S) SS *Prince Charles*]

LSI(S) Unit
LSI(S) SS *Prince Baudoin*	(5th Rangers – part)
LSI(S) SS *Prince Charles*	(2nd Rangers – part)
LSI(S) SS *Prince Leopold*	(5th Rangers – part)

LSI(H) Unit
LSI(H) SS *Ben My Chree*	(2nd Rangers – part)
LSI(H) SS *Amsterdam*	(2nd Rangers – part)
LSI(H) SS *Princess Maud*	(Special Engineer Task Force)

Task Force O Support Group *Captain L.S. Sabin, USN* [*LCI(L) 520*]
5 x LCG (Large); 9 x LCT (Rocket); 7 x LCF; 8 x LCT (Armoured);
10 x LCT (High Explosive); 28 LCP(L) Smoke

Bombarding Force C
Major warships detailed separately on page 56

Patrol Craft
PC 552, PC 553, PC 564, PC 565, PC 576, PC 568, PC 617, PC 618.

Anti-Submarine Trawlers
HMS *Bressay*; HMS *Coll*, HMS *Sky*

Minesweeper Group   *Commander J.S. Cochrane, RN* [HMS *Kellett*]
Sweep Unit 1 (4th Minesweeper Flotilla – all British ships) *Cdr Cochrane*
    Kellett, Albury, Elgin, Lydd, Pangbourne, Ross, Saltash, Selkirk, Sutton
Sweep Unit 2 (31st Minesweeper Flotilla – all Canadian ships)
    Commander A.H.G. Storrs, RCNR [HMCS *Caraquet*]
    Caraquet, Blairmore, Cowichan, Fort William, Malpeque, Milltown,
    Minas, Mulgrave, Wasaga,
Sweep Unit 3 (167th Minesweeper Flotilla)
    BYMSs 2050, 2061, 2069, 2154, 2155, 2156, 2182, 2210, 2255, 2256
Sweep Unit 4 (104th Minesweeper Flotilla)
    MMSs 75, 31, 37, 74, 84, 86, 260, 279, 280, 305
Attached motor launches: MLs 118, 153, 163, 187, 189, 194, 214, 230,
    448, 907, HDML 1383, HDML 1387

NB: The US Army official history *Omaha Beachhead* gives a total of 1,028 vessels in
Task Force O including landing craft. Also, many ships and craft carried out roles for
the Western Task Force or for the Allied naval forces generally rather than as part of
Task Force O, including salvage vessels, depot and repair ships, ancillary ships, etc.

Key: AGC Headquarters Ship; APA Attack Transport; AP Transport (modified for
attack); BYMS British Yard Mine Sweeper; HDML Harbour Defence Motor Launch;
LCA Landing Craft Assault; LCC Landing Craft Control; LCF Landing Craft Flak;
LCG(L) Landing Craft Gun (Large); LCH Landing Craft Headquarters; LCM Landing
Craft Mechanised; LCI(L) Landing Craft Infantry (Large); LCI(S) Landing Craft
Infantry (Small); LCP(L) Landing Craft Personnel (Large); LCS Landing Craft Support;
LCT Landing Craft Tank; LCVP Landing Craft Vehicle Personnel; LSD Landing Ship
Dock; LSI(H) Landing Ship Infantry (Hand-Hoist); LSI(L) Landing Ship Infantry (Large);
LSI(S) Landing Ship Infantry (Small); ML Motor Launch; MMS Motor Minesweeper.

Sources: [Commander L.J. Pitcairn-Jones RN], *Operation 'Neptune': The Landings in
Normandy 6th June 1944* British Naval Staff History Battle Summary Number 39.
S.E. Morison, *The Invasion of France and Germany 1944–1945*, History of United
States Naval Operations in World War II.

GIs boarding
LCI 539 from an
LCVP. Probably
before 6 June.
(IWM EN25384)

By 0055 hours British and Canadian minesweepers had swept the Transport Area off Omaha Beach, starting just over 21 km offshore in Area Elder, and then began sweeping towards the Line of Departure for the landing craft, and the sea on either side for the heavy warships: Fire Support Area Three to the west and Fire Support Area Four to the east. By 0615 hours this work was completed and the sun was up in a partially overcast sky; no mines were found. Arriving in the Transport Area at 0220 hours, the big warships deployed to their firing stations as the mine-sweepers cleared them.

USS *Ancon*, the command ship for Task Force O, anchored at 0251 hours with Rear Admiral Hall and Maj Gen Gerow on board, followed by the cruiser USS *Augusta*, flagship of the Western Task Force, with Admiral Kirk and Lt Gen Bradley. Shortly afterwards the assault landing ships began to embark their troops into landing craft. Other than the *Ancon*, there were 15 assault landing ships with Task Force O. Assault Groups O1 to O3 had between them seven American assault ships, typically each carrying 1,400 troops and 26 LCVPs (Landing Craft

Vehicle Personnel, also known as 'Higgins Boats' from their designer Andrew Jackson Higgins), each one carrying a 'boat team' or 'boat section' of 30–36 men. Landing craft were crewed by the US Navy and Coast Guard. In the still-segregated US armed forces, some men noted if the coxswain of their boat was African-American, 'colored' or 'negro' in the language of the time.

Assault Groups O1 and O2 also each included a British Landing Ship Infantry (Large) with 900–1,400 troops and 18 LCAs (Landing Craft Assault) crewed by the Royal Navy. Assault Group O4 was composed of six smaller British ships, three Landing Ships Infantry (Small) converted from Belgian cross-Channel ferries, and three Landing Ships Infantry (Hand-Hoist) – from their method of loading troops – each carrying about 200–250 troops and 8 LCA. These were supported by 24 Landing Ships Tank (LST), each holding a company of infantry or the equivalent, and by other specialist landing craft.

Because of the poor sea conditions, landing craft were despatched to the Line of Departure ahead of schedule as soon as they had embarked their troops, mostly before 0430 hours, in an effort to minimise delay. In darkness and rain, the flat-bottomed boats skidded and slipped around the larger ships, including the battleships and cruisers moving to their firing positions. The LCVPs and LCAs began to ship water almost at once, and at least 10 foundered and sank; many smaller DUKW ('duck craft'), amphibious trucks carrying equipment and guns, could not launch at all. At the Line of Departure the landing craft formed up and kept station until signalled forward to the beach by lights from Landing Craft Control (LCC), equipped with radar and captained by members of the US Navy's Scouts and Raiders, specialists in amphibious operations, while US Navy PT boats (fast torpedo boats) and Patrol Craft (PC) policed the edges of the landing area. Then, fighting the wind and current and still shipping water, the landing craft pressed on for the beach carrying their cold, wet, heavily burdened and mostly seasick soldiers.

NAVAL BOMBARDMENT OF OMAHA BEACH DEFENCES

Bombarding Force C *Rear Admiral C.F. Bryant*, USN [USS *Texas*]

Ship	Main armament	Principal targets
USS *Texas* (battleship)	10 x 14-inch, 6 x 5-inch	Pointe du Hoc, Vierville draw (Dog-1)
USS *Arkansas* (battleship)	12 x 12-inch, 6 x 5-inch	Longues Battery, les Moulins area
HMS *Glasgow* (cruiser)	12 x 6-inch	les Moulins defences, Grandcamp area
FFS *Montcalm* (cruiser)	9 x 6-inch	Port-en-Bessin, western Omaha defences
FFS *Georges Leygues* (cruiser)	9 x 6-inch	Colleville draw (Easy-3)
USS *McCook* (destroyer)	4 x 5-inch	Vierville defences
USS *Carmick* (destroyer)	4 x 5-inch	les Moulins defences
USS *Doyle* (destroyer)	4 x 5-inch	Fox Green defences, Port-en-Bessin, Easy Red area
USS *Emmons* (destroyer)	4 x 5-inch	Fox Green defences, Colleville-sur-Mer village
USS *Baldwin* (destroyer)	4 x 5-inch	Fox Green defences, Easy Sector area
USS *Harding* (destroyer)	4 x 5-inch	Fox Green defences, Pointe du Hoc
USS *Satterlee* (destroyer)	4 x 5-inch	Pointe du Hoc
USS *Thompson* (destroyer)	4 x 5-inch	Pointe et Raz de la Percée, Easy Red, les Moulins
HMS *Tanatside* (destroyer)	4 x 4-inch	Colleville draw (Easy-3)
HMS *Talybont* (destroyer)	4 x 4-inch	Pointe et Raz de la Percée, Pointe du Hoc
HMS *Melbreak* (destroyer)	4 x 4-inch	Ste-Honorine-des-Pertes
USS *Barton* (destroyer)	4 x 5-inch	Pointe du Hoc
USS *Frankford* (destroyer)	4 x 5-inch	Fox Green area

Notes

All these vessels were part of Bombarding Force C except USS *Barton* (committed from the reserve) and USS *Frankford* (from the anti-submarine screening force).
The following major warships were also part of Task Force O, but do not appear to have played any role in the beach bombardment: HMS *Bellona* (cruiser, 8 x 5.25-inch); British destroyers *Vesper* and *Vidette*; US destroyers *Amesbury*, *Blessman*, *Borum*, *Laffey*, *Meredeth*, *O'Brien*, *Plunkett*, and *Walke*.

At 0502 hours in the half-light just before dawn, 352nd Infantry Division's resistance nests at Port-en-Bessin reported Allied ships off the coast, and at 0530 hours their field guns opened fire on the destroyer USS *Emmons*, with other batteries to the east joining in, including the Longues battery with its two westernmost guns. Fire was returned first by the *Emmons* and by one of two French cruisers off Omaha, the *Georges Leygues*. With the dawn coming,

Supermarine Spitfire spotter aircraft arrived over the beach, flown by the RAF and Royal Navy and US Navy Squadron VCS-7 (specially formed for the invasion), and the battleship USS *Arkansas* also returned fire, briefly silencing the German guns by 0552 hours. The Longues battery opened fire again on the ships in Fire Support Area Four at 0605 hours, and the second French cruiser *Montcalm* replied, as did the British cruiser HMS *Ajax* off Gold Beach, again silencing the battery. Meanwhile the cruiser HMS *Hawkins* off Utah Beach commenced bombardment of the German batteries near Maisy, inflicting heavy casualties on III/726th Grenadiers defending the area and reducing the village largely to rubble. The battery at Longues did not open fire on the ships off Omaha again until 1700 hours, when it was once more silenced by the two French cruisers and by the *Ajax*.

The planned shore bombardment at Omaha began at 0550 hours. The most importantly rated target was the Pointe du Hoc battery, which was blasted by the 14-inch guns of the USS *Texas*. The radar station on the Pointe et Raz de la Percée was destroyed by shells from the destroyer HMS *Talybont*, which then joined the destroyer USS *Satterlee* in firing at the Pointe du Hoc. At 0552 hours USS *Arkansas* switched its main armament to WN-68 and WN-66 at Dog-3, commencing what was known as 'beach drenching'. Most of the naval gunnery at Omaha went into saturating the resistance nests along the beach and on the bluffs, with the destroyers coming as close as 2,200 metres to the shore, supplemented by fire from the landing craft as they drew closer to the beach. It was a terrifying experience; some German soldiers endured it, some prayed openly for their lives as the shells fell around them, others never reached their positions or, according to French eyewitnesses, fled to avoid the shelling.

From dawn at 0556 hours onwards a rotating Allied air plan provided six RAF Spitfire squadrons for low cover over the beach areas and three squadrons of USAAF Republic P-47 Thunderbolts for high cover, with a further Thunderbolt squadron covering Western Task Force,

The Allied bombardment of Omaha Beach caused considerable damage to the buildings along the seafront between Colleville and Vierville-sur-Mer. Here, two GIs pass a destroyed house beside the coastal road near les Moulins. (USNA)

and a Spitfire squadron assigned to each of Utah and Omaha Beaches. Four squadrons of distinctive twin-boomed USAAF Lockheed P-38 Lightning fighters, which could not be mistaken for German aircraft, flew cover over the Channel convoys. As a further precaution, all Allied aircraft were painted for D-Day with 'Invasion Stripes', black and white bands across the wings and around the fuselage. Also at 0556 hours, 448 B-24 Liberators of 2nd Bombardment Division returned to drop 1,300 tonnes (1,430 US tons) of bombs onto the Omaha Beach defences. Bombing through the overcast and told to leave a safety margin of 1,000 metres, the bomb aimers mostly overshot by up to 5 km to hit the empty fields beyond the bluffs; 117 Liberators brought their bombs home, unable to see their targets. Only three bombs fell near the beach area, one close to the rear of WN-62, inflicting no major damage.

At 0600 hours, as part of the beach drenching, 36 M7 Priest 105-mm self-propelled howitzers of 58th and 62nd Armored Field Artillery Battalions, carried by 10 LCTs, opened fire from 8,000 metres, closing to 3,400 metres from the beach. Ten minutes later, five LCG(L)s

(Landing Craft Gun – Large) each joined in with their two 4.7-inch guns. On 16 LCTs each carrying two M4 Sherman tanks, either from A Company, 741st Tank Battalion, (A/741st Tank Battalion) or from A/743rd Tank Battalion, together with a tankdozer for the demolition teams, the tanks opened fire from 3,000 metres at 0615 hours. On the beach, II/916th Grenadiers reported its resistance nests under fire at 0604 hours, and under 'particularly heavy fire' ten minutes later, with WN-60 near Fox-1 very badly hit. As a last contribution, from 0623 to 0632 hours nine LCT(R)s each discharged 1,064 5-inch rockets from 3,000 metres offshore onto the beach, the first planned to hit when the LCVPs were only 300 metres from touchdown. Many American soldiers remembered these rockets falling short into the sea or shooting wildly overhead, but most apparently fell on their intended target areas. Possibly, some German rockets from WN-67, arcing over the bluffs and splashing down around the incoming landing craft, were mistaken for friendly fire.

For the landings the American regiments, led by 16th Infantry under Colonel (Col) George A. Taylor and 116th Infantry under Col Charles D.W. Canham, were organised into Regimental Combat Teams (RCT) by the addition of specialist demolition troops and heavy weapons; a typical Assault Boat Team in an LCVP carried flame-throwers, 60-mm mortars, bazookas and wire-cutters. The plan called

The destroyer USS *Thompson*, photographed in May 1944. The *Thompson* provided effective direct fire support to V Corps' units on D-Day, especially against German beach defences at and around les Moulins. *(USNA)*

A mixture of fear, apprehension and resolve marks the faces of these infantrymen and their Coast Guard crew as their LCVP prepares to head in towards the beach on the morning of 6 June. *(USNA)*

for 64 amphibious Sherman DD tanks (for 'Duplex Drive', fitted with propellers and waterproofing) of B/743rd and C/743rd Tank Battalion with 116th RCT, together with B/741st and C/741st Tank Battalion with 16th RCT, to launch 6,000 metres offshore at 0550 hours and swim onto the beach at 0625 hours, followed at 0630 hours by A/743rd Tank Battalion and A/741st Tank Battalion landing from their LCTs. If all went to plan, a minute later the first infantry wave from each RCT, a total of 1,450 men, would land to find 96 friendly tanks ready to help them. Companies A, E, F and G/116th RCT launched from AP 30 *Thomas Jefferson* and LSI(L) *Empire Javelin*; Companies E, F, I and L/16th RCT launched from APA 45 *Henrico* and LSI(L) *Empire Anvil*. The demolition teams and engineers from 146th Engineer Combat Battalion (ECB) and 299th ECB would land three minutes later, followed at 0700 hours by the succeeding lines of troops from each infantry battalion. Thereafter from 0710 to 1015 hours, 13 more lines of landing craft would come ashore at varying intervals to complete the landing by 16th RCT and 116th RCT.

Launching in LCAs from the LSI(H) *Amsterdam* and *Ben My Chree*, Lt Col Rudder's force of 225 men, Companies D, E and F/2nd Rangers, set out for the cliffs at the Pointe du

Hoc planning to land at 0630 hours. The plan also called for Company C, 2nd Rangers, to land at Dog Green Beach from LSI(S) *Prince Charles* at 0633 hours with 116th RCT, and to move quickly off the beach to capture the radar station on the Pointe et Raz de la Percée. If by 0700 hours Rudder's men had signalled success, 5th Rangers and the rest of 2nd Rangers would land at the Pointe du Hoc as reinforcements. If not, they would land at Dog Green and follow up C/2nd Rangers to reach the Pointe du Hoc by the coast road.

There were later claims that Lt Col Rudder knew when he launched his attack on the Pointe du Hoc that the 155-mm guns of 2/1260th Coastal Artillery were not in their casemates; but since the guns were mobile this did not matter, they had to be found and destroyed. The wind and current, and difficulties identifying landmarks, took the Rangers eastward almost to the Point et Raz de la Percée before the error was corrected. Instead of landing at the foot of the cliffs on either side of the Pointe du Hoc, all three companies landed on the eastern side at 0708 hours, too late to signal success to their reinforcements. Greatly assisted by shellfire from the *Talybont* and the *Satterlee*, of which they were largely unaware, the Rangers scaled the cliffs under fire, overcame the German defenders who had survived the earlier bombardment from air and sea, and attacked the empty gun casemates and surrounding entrenchments. Continuing rapidly inland through the heavily cratered *Stützpunkt*, and by-passing some of its defenders, the Rangers set up a blocking position across the clifftop road, all within an hour of landing. Shortly afterwards they came under the first of several counter-attacks, by a platoon of 9/726th Grenadiers. By 0900 hours the Rangers had found the abandoned but undamaged German battery in temporary defences 1,500 metres inland, and disabled its guns. Having signalled success, for the rest of the day they found themselves under increasing German fire, supported only by the destroyers offshore. At 1723 hours USS *Satterlee* recorded having fired 164 salvoes plus emergency fire, and had expended 70 per cent of its ammunition.

One of the unprotected emplacements for the 155-mm guns stationed on the Pointe du Hoc. The two enclosed casemates can be seen on the horizon to the left and right. The exposed nature of most of the guns' positions was the reason for them being held inland to avoid destruction by Allied air attacks made in the weeks prior to 6 June. (David Nairn [DN])

Like Rudder's force of Rangers, the flat-bottomed LCVPs and LCAs leaving the Line of Departure for Omaha Beach were pushed off course eastward by the strong wind and current, and had difficulties locating their landing points. The beach area was covered with dust and smoke from the bombardment, which had set the undergrowth on the bluffs alight, and as the landing craft approached the shore both formations and timings began to break apart. There was little German shellfire; the 105-mm guns of I/352nd Artillery did not have the range to fire on these fast-moving targets out to sea, and only 10 landing craft were hit, none of them sunk. But unknown to the Americans both the resistance nests and their heavy weapons were still largely intact, as were I/352nd Artillery and elements of 84th Rocket Launcher Regiment supporting them. The final bombing from the air had failed, and although later Allied analysis judged the beach drenching at Omaha only marginally less powerful than on the other landing beaches, the random fall of shells and rockets had simply missed or failed to destroy its most important targets.

CHAPTER 4

BLOODY OMAHA

What happened on Omaha Beach in the next few hours has been analysed and reconstructed many times, from official records and from personal memories, not always to the satisfaction of those who were there. On the German side, the artillery spotters in WN-62, the company headquarters in WN-63 at Colleville, and observers on the Pointe et Raz de la Percée telephoned back what they could see during the day. The first American troops ashore on Omaha, and the first casualties, were probably Gap Assault Team 14 of the Special Engineer Task Force landing early at 0625 hours on Easy Red beach, most of whom were killed or wounded as the Germans opened fire and their landing craft exploded. Other Gap Assault Teams, having hit problems either in the Channel crossing or the Transport Area, landed out of position and sometimes before their accompanying infantry, taking heavy casualties and losing equipment.

Given the height of the waves and the low freeboard of the 32-ton DD Sherman tanks, launching them became a dangerous decision. On leaving the Transport Area Lieutenant (Lt) Dean L. Rockwell, USNR, commanding patrol craft PC-568 guided in the LCTs for 116th RCT, assigning those for 16th RCT to control craft LCC 20, accompanied by PC-552. Rather than risk launching their tanks into the swell, Rockwell's LCTs circled until the LCTs carrying A/743rd Tank Battalion caught up, and all three companies of the battalion then landed together on the western half of the beach. B/743rd Tank Battalion, landing opposite Dog-1, lost its company commander and

On fire after being hit, an LCVP from the attack transport *Samuel Chase* approaches the shoreline early on 6 June. Beach obstacles can be seen in the background, as can the Omaha bluffs, barely visible behind the smoke and haze caused by the preliminary bombardment. *(USNA)*

half its tanks to artillery on the approach or at the water's edge. The remaining tanks opened fire, but could not get across the shingle bank.

In 16th RCT's sector to the east, one of the LCTs carrying the DD Shermans strayed off course on the approach, but the others delayed their moment of launch only slightly to within 5,000 metres of the beach, still in darkness. Within minutes the tanks began to swamp and the crews had to swim for their lives. Only two swam onto Fox Green and three could not launch because of a damaged ramp; the remaining 27 sank, although most of their crews survived. One tank at once engaged the 75-mm gun at WN-60. A/741st Tank Battalion, landing from its LCTs, lost two tanks before the shore and three more on landing. This left the arriving troops of 16th RCT almost without armour support.

The first lines of LCVPs carrying 16th RCT reached the beach before 0632 hours, and those carrying 116th RCT a little later. As the successive lines of landing craft approached their touch-down points they were fired upon in turn by the German artillery and heavy weapons. 'The enemy would wait until the craft lowered their ramps,' one junior US Navy officer remembered, 'and then cut loose with everything they had.' Within minutes the American assault had disintegrated into chaos in the face of shells, mortars, and machine guns. At Vierville where Dog-1 draw formed a conspicuous landmark, Company A/116th RCT was effectively wiped out at the water's edge: one of its six British LCAs swamped on the approach, and every officer and most of the sergeants were killed or wounded. Company C, 2nd Rangers, landing at 0645 hours on Charlie Beach to the west, lost 37 out of 68 men in the landing and the survivors then took refuge at the foot of the 30-metre cliffs.

Many of the other landing craft steered or drifted well east of their objectives. There was a long gap across the front of WN-70 at Hamel au Prêtre before the next landing, by F/116th and G/116th RCT opposite Dog-3 at les Moulins. Most of the first wave from both regiments actually came ashore in 16th RCT's sector: E/16th RCT and part of E/116th RCT on Easy Red through the gap in the Belgian gates, and a jumble of boats carrying troops from E and F/16th RCT and E/116th RCT on Fox Green in front of Easy-3. Only two out of eight companies, the hard-hit A/116th RCT and most of F/116th RCT, landed on their target beaches. Among those landing was the war photographer Robert Capa, who took some famous pictures. The best landing was made by L/16th RCT touching down late at about 0700 hours, out of position in the dead ground at the foot of the cliffs on Fox Red, having lost two landing craft but, unlike the other seven companies in the first wave, still together as a unit with 125 men.

One of the most famous of all D-Day images, photographed by Robert Capa. Men from E/16th RCT struggle through the shallows on Easy Red soon after 0630 hours. Despite the blurring in the photograph, beach obstacles and men either hit or taking cover in the water can all be seen clearly. (IWM HU53296)

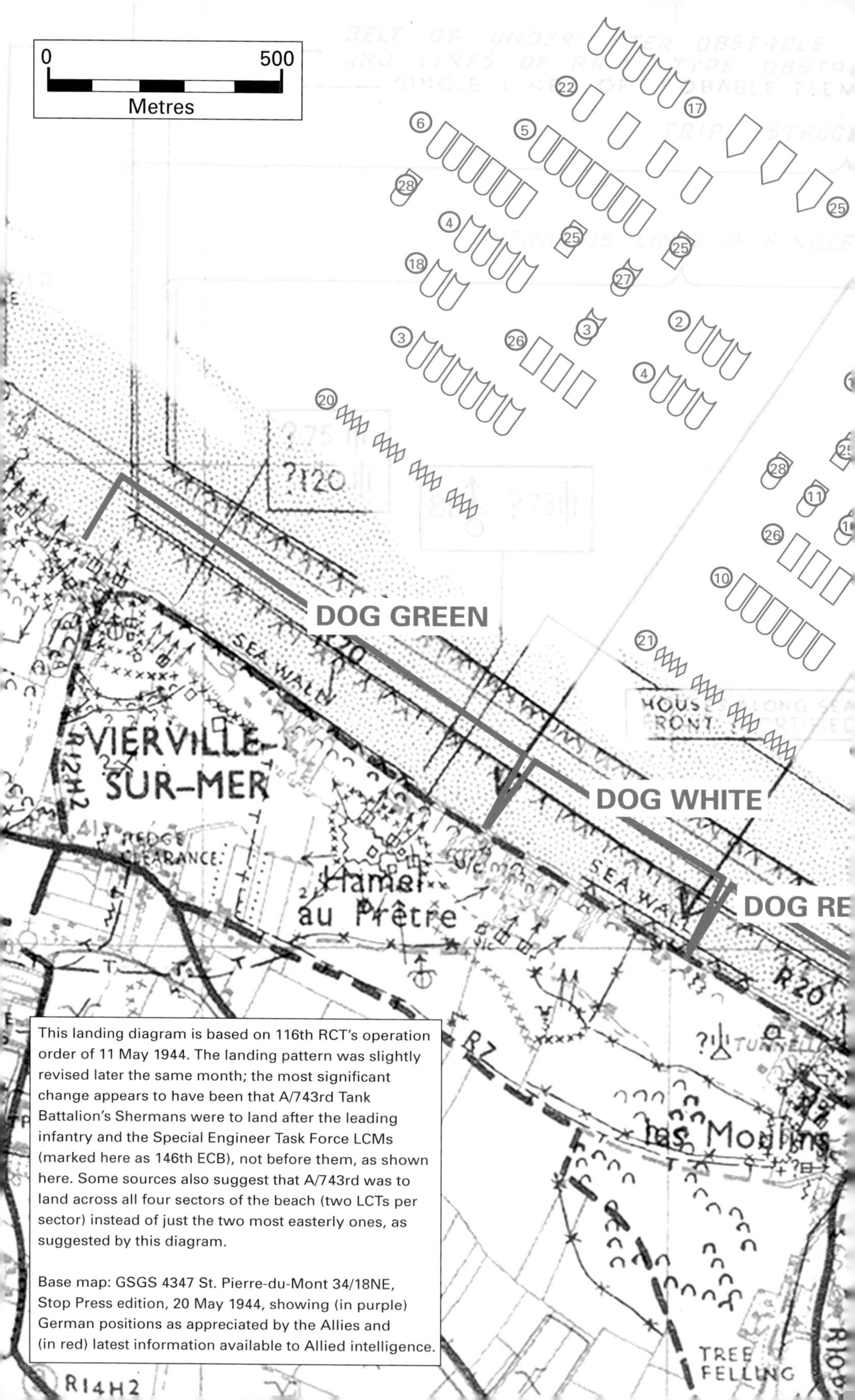
0
500
Metres
DOG GREEN
DOG WHITE
DOG RE
VIERVILLE-SUR-MER
Hamel au Prêtre
SEA WALL
SEA WALL
R20
R20
?120
?275
R12H2
HEDGE CLEARANCE
R14H2
TREE FELLING
R10
les Moulins
TUNNEL
HOUSES ALONG SEA FRONT FORTIFIED

This landing diagram is based on 116th RCT's operation order of 11 May 1944. The landing pattern was slightly revised later the same month; the most significant change appears to have been that A/743rd Tank Battalion's Shermans were to land after the leading infantry and the Special Engineer Task Force LCMs (marked here as 146th ECB), not before them, as shown here. Some sources also suggest that A/743rd was to land across all four sectors of the beach (two LCTs per sector) instead of just the two most easterly ones, as suggested by this diagram.

Base map: GSGS 4347 St. Pierre-du-Mont 34/18NE, Stop Press edition, 20 May 1944, showing (in purple) German positions as appreciated by the Allies and (in red) latest information available to Allied intelligence.

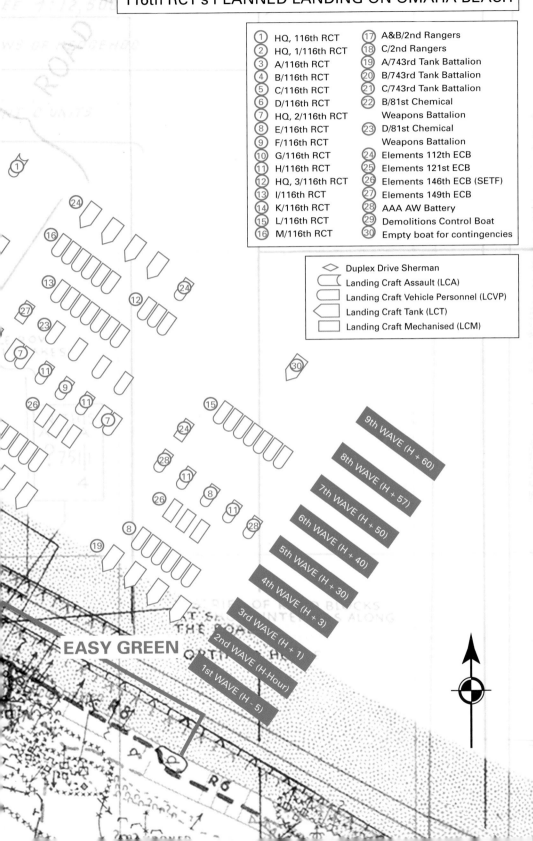

116th RCT's PLANNED LANDING ON OMAHA BEACH

1. HQ, 116th RCT
2. HQ, 1/116th RCT
3. A/116th RCT
4. B/116th RCT
5. C/116th RCT
6. D/116th RCT
7. HQ, 2/116th RCT
8. E/116th RCT
9. F/116th RCT
10. G/116th RCT
11. H/116th RCT
12. HQ, 3/116th RCT
13. I/116th RCT
14. K/116th RCT
15. L/116th RCT
16. M/116th RCT
17. A&B/2nd Rangers
18. C/2nd Rangers
19. A/743rd Tank Battalion
20. B/743rd Tank Battalion
21. C/743rd Tank Battalion
22. B/81st Chemical Weapons Battalion
23. D/81st Chemical Weapons Battalion
24. Elements 112th ECB
25. Elements 121st ECB
26. Elements 146th ECB (SETF)
27. Elements 149th ECB
28. AAA AW Battery
29. Demolitions Control Boat
30. Empty boat for contingencies

◇ Duplex Drive Sherman
⌐ Landing Craft Assault (LCA)
⌐ Landing Craft Vehicle Personnel (LCVP)
◁ Landing Craft Tank (LCT)
▭ Landing Craft Mechanised (LCM)

9th WAVE (H + 60)
8th WAVE (H + 57)
7th WAVE (H + 50)
6th WAVE (H + 50)
5th WAVE (H + 40)
4th WAVE (H + 30)
3rd WAVE (H + 3)
2nd WAVE (H + 1)
1st WAVE (H-Hour)
1st WAVE (H - 5)

EASY GREEN

Most of the soldiers who made it out of their landing craft were already too seasick, soaked, cramped and exhausted even to run; many took refuge among the beach obstacles, preventing the specialist engineers from blowing them up. Others pressed or crawled forward to the comparative safety of the concrete seawall or the shingle bank. Caught in the crossfire from WN-66 and WN-68, some troops of 2/116th RCT at les Moulins, estimated by the defenders of WN-68 as no more than 50 men, took 45 minutes to work their way to the seawall. A litter of bodies covered the sand, and many of those who stayed beside the obstacles were wounded by shells or bullets, and slumped down and drowned in the shallow water. Equipment and heavy weapons were lost, including vital demolition gear, and even rifles clogged with sand. Most of the Navy's Shore Fire Control Parties did not get ashore, or did not survive to direct the naval gunnery onto the resistance nests. Three-quarters of all 116th RCT's radios were damaged or destroyed. The first of three Medal of Honor winners on Omaha Beach on D-Day was Technician John J. Pinder Jr. of 16th Infantry, who went back into the bullet-swept surf three times to rescue radio equipment and get it working, finally dying of his wounds. At 0641 hours, the patrol craft PC-552 signalled back to the *Samuel Chase*, 'entire first wave foundered'.

V CORPS ENGINEER UNITS ON OMAHA BEACH

Special Engineer Task Force   *Colonel John O'Neill*

16 gap assault teams and 8 support teams, comprising elements from:
146th Engineer Combat Battalion   *Lt Col Carl J. Isley*
299th Engineer Combat Btn (less B Coy)   *Major Jewitt*
21 Naval Combat Demolition Unit (NCDU) teams*

* Plus 16 attached tankdozers from 741st and 743rd Tank Battalions and
  610th Engineer Light Equipment Company

Provisional Engineer Special Brigade Group
                                        Brig Gen William M. Hoge
Assistant Group Commander: *Colonel Timothy L. Mulligan*

5th Engineer Special Brigade   ***Colonel Doswell Gullatt***

37th Engineer Combat Battalion   *Lt Col Lionel F. Smith (KIA 6/6)*
                                        then Major John E. Gottschalk

336th Engineer Combat Battalion   *Lt Col Paul D. Bennett*
348th Engineer Combat Battalion   *Lt Col Earl P. Houston*
533rd Quartermaster Service Battalion, 619th Quartermaster Battalion,
131st Quartermaster Mobile Battalion,   251st Ordnance Battalion,
61st Medical Battalion, 210th Military Police Company,
294th Joint Assault Signal Company, 487th Port Battalion*,
6th Naval Beach Battalion*, 502nd Port Battalion*

6th Engineer Special Brigade   ***Colonel Paul W. Thompson***

147th Engineer Combat Battalion   *Lt Col James F. Neill*
149th Engineer Combat Battalion   *Lt Col James C. Taylor*
203rd Engineer Combat Battalion   *Lt Col Ira O. Thorley Jr.*
538th Quartermaster Service Battalion, 95th Quartermaster Battalion,
280th Quartermaster Battalion, 74th Ordnance Battalion,
60th Medical Battalion, 214th Military Police Company,
293rd Joint Assault Signal Company, 7th Naval Beach Battalion*,
494th Port Battalion*, 517th Port Battalion*

*Attached units. Numerous smaller specialist units attached to both brigades.

11th Port   ***Colonel Richard S. Whitcomb***

501st Port Battalion; 509th Port Battalion; 514th Port Battalion;
688th Quartermaster Service Battalion; 556th Quartermaster Service
Battalion; 554th Quartermaster Service Battalion; 512th Quartermaster
Battalion; 174th Quartermaster Battalion and other small specialist units.

The next lines of landing craft, carrying infantry, engineers and mortar crews, were due to land at 0700–0710 hours. Because of the bad weather the tide was rising higher than expected and starting to cover the obstacles; the Belgian gates were already under water. Only five of the gap assault teams had landed where expected. Only six tankdozers got onto the beach; three were hit almost immediately. The survivors gathered their remaining explosives and tried to clear lanes 50–100 metres wide through the obstacles to let the landing craft through, working in the open under heavy fire. The Navy Combat Demolition Unit received a Presidential Unit Citation for its work on D-Day. The first lane was blown at 0655 hours, and in all five lanes and three partial lanes were blasted through the obstacles, the widest gaps being on Easy Red, making a precarious path from the gap in the Belgian gates to the dead ground at the foot of the bluff between WN-62 and WN-64. But none of the lanes could be clearly marked. As the landing craft approached they were signalled away from the uncleared sections of beach and began to circle around just offshore, exposed to German fire. Some tried to find their way inshore but became stuck on the obstacles and blew up on the mines or were sunk by German shells. At 0725 hours WN-61 reported destroying a landing craft with its 50-mm anti-tank gun.

As had happened to the first landings, the troops of the succeeding waves coming in opposite Vierville were most successful in locating their target beaches. Having received no signal from Lt Col Rudder at the Pointe du Hoc by 0710 hours, A/ and B/2nd Rangers landed on Dog Green, with 5th Rangers veering eastward to land on Dog White. Again, companies landed to the east of their planned positions, and troops of 116th RCT ended up scattered across the boundary line between the two regiments. Many soldiers had no idea where they were, and were far away from their equipment or their planned objectives. Rather than advancing inland, some tried to reach their correct sectors thousands of metres away along the bullet-swept beach. Among those who got ashore by 0730 hours were Brig Gen Cota and Col Canham, commanding 116th RCT, landing on Dog White. The largest single group of landings again took place through the gaps blown in the obstacles in front of the dead ground between WN-62 and WN-64, where men of at least five companies of 1/16th RCT and 2/16th RCT reached the safety of the shingle bank, all mixed together. Col Taylor, commanding 16th RCT, joined his men on the beach at 0815 hours. Two companies of 3/16th RCT landed at Fox Green, again reinforcing the

earlier landing. These included I/16th RCT, whose LCVPs had overshot to the east almost as far as Port-en-Bessin before turning back and landing at 0800 hours. By then both 16th RCT and 116th RCT were ashore, six battalions in all plus the two regimental headquarters; but although luck varied between the infantry companies, most had taken at least 50–60 casualties.

The Americans were now in a terrible trap. Their smaller craft could not make the journey from the Transport Area without swamping, and the bigger ones could not get inshore past the German beach defences, by then completely under water up to the last line of hedgehogs. At least 50 LCTs and LCIs (Landing Craft Infantry) circled just offshore, looking for a way through the submerged beach defences. LCI 91 and LCI 92, coming into Dog White beach a few minutes apart at 0740 hours, both either hit mines or were hit by shells or rockets; the two big craft burned for hours. Some landing craft that successfully navigated the obstacles grounded on sandbars, leaving their soldiers to cover more than 200 metres of shallows and beach under fire.

The Sherman tanks that had made it to the beach could fight, but only move with difficulty and at high risk, and they had little support. Although mortar crews of 81st Chemical Weapons Battalion ('chemical' because its 4.2-inch mortars had originally been intended for smoke) landed with the second wave, several mortars and their ammunition were lost; 397th Anti-Aircraft Artillery Automatic Weapons Battalion with 16th RCT lost 29 of its

In another of the sequence taken by the *LIFE* photographer Robert Capa, US infantry cross an offshore sandbar at Omaha Beach early on 6 June. Visible in the background are troops nearer the shore (but in deeper water), steel hedgehogs and several Sherman tanks. Many of the troops are hiding in the shallows, behind the tanks, or at the pebble bank near the top of the beach. *(IWM AP25726)*

ANTI-AIRCRAFT ARTILLERY UNITS ON OMAHA BEACH

First US Army Assets

49th AAA Brigade (elements)
320th Barrage Balloon Battalion (Very Low Altitude) (elements)
16th AAA Group
    413th AAA Gun Battalion; 197th & 457th AAA AW Battalions
18th AAA Group
    110th AAA Gun Battalion; 447th AAA AW Battalion;
    467th AAA AW Battalion (Self-Propelled)

US V Corps Assets

103rd AAA AW Battalion *(supporting 1st Infantry Division)*
459th AAA AW Battalion *(supporting 29th Infantry Division)*
115th AAA Group
    430th, 460th, 462nd AAA Battalions

Note
AAA Anti-Aircraft Artillery; AW Automatic Weapons.
AAA gun battalions were equipped with 16 x 90-mm guns and 16 x .50-calibre machine guns.
AAA AW battalions were armed with 32 x M51 quad .50-calibre machine guns, 32 x 40-mm guns and 32 x water-cooled machine guns.
Self-Propelled AW battalions had 32 half-tracks armed with an M15 37-mm and twin 50-cal machine guns and 32 half-tracks armed with quad .50-calibre machine guns.

36 heavy machine guns disembarking; all 13 DUKW craft meant to bring in the 105-mm howitzers of 111th Field Artillery Battalion at 0800 hours swamped or were sunk, and only one howitzer made it ashore; 7th Field Artillery Battalion fared little better, losing six howitzers when their DUKWs swamped and being unable to land the others; DUKWs bringing in the six howitzers of 16th RCT Cannon Company all swamped out at sea; the M7 Priests of 58th and 62nd Armored Field Artillery Battalions in their LCTs were lost out at sea or could not land. Almost all the heavy firepower needed to overcome the German defences therefore had to come from the ships offshore, but from 5,000 metres the beach was only a narrow ribbon of sand wreathed in smoke. At about 0830 hours a beachmaster from 7th Naval Beach Battalion signalled the LCCs to suspend the landing of vehicles. At 0945 hours V Corps made its first report to First Army, 'Obstacles mined, progress slow'. After receiving equally disturbing reports from his own staff officers offshore closer to the beach, on board the USS *Augusta* Lt Gen Bradley began to wonder if there was any way to save the troops, and evacuate Omaha altogether.

CHAPTER 5

BEYOND THE BLUFFS

There was no one single climactic moment at which the battle for Omaha Beach was won and lost. For the Americans at the foot of the bluffs and along the shingle bank there was no choice but to advance. In a resounding phrase attributed to Col Canham, 'They're murdering us here – let's move inland and get murdered!' So thick was the smoke from the burning undergrowth, blowing particularly between WN-68 and WN-70, that some men described donning their gas masks for protection. The beach drenching had blown gaps through the wire and minefields along the sand and on top of the bluffs, including some sections of dead ground. Small groups of American soldiers began to work their way by ones and twos uphill, unseen heroes who sometimes did not survive. Despite their firepower, several of the German resistance nests were also seriously undermanned. The giant WN-62 position at Easy-3 held only 31 men including the seven spotters from 1/352nd Artillery, leaving 24 soldiers to crew seven heavy weapons and to defend the perimeter. WN-61 to the west of the Fox-1 draw had only 12 defenders, and its 88-mm gun was destroyed at 0710 hours, probably by a shell from a DD Sherman. The numbers at WN-71 and WN-73 defending Dog-1 were also recorded as very weak. Perhaps fewer than 500 German soldiers were present on Omaha Beach, and every casualty meant a gap in the line. As early as 0735 hours, 3/726th Grenadiers reported that 100–200 American troops had penetrated its front, that the enemy were inside the wire at WN-62, and that WN-61 was under attack from the rear.

At 0800 hours the eight American and three shallower-draft British 'Hunt' class destroyers of the bombardment force closed inshore to select their own targets according to plan, and at 0948 hours USS *McCook* destroyed a 75-mm gun position built into the cliff, part of WN-74, that had been firing on the troops at Dog-1. Two minutes later, Rear Admiral Bryant in charge of the bombardment force ordered the destroyers to get as close into the beach as possible; some came in to 900 metres, past the three fathom line (5.5 metres deep) several times, risking running aground as they scraped along the seabed. At this range, the destroyer captains could see where tanks and infantry were shooting and directed their own gunfire in support. By 1045 hours at least one Shore Fire Control Party was back in action. The USS *Arkansas* continued to fire towards Port-en-Bessin and to the east of Omaha, but with success announced from the Pointe du Hoc, USS *Texas* was free to use its 14-inch main armament against the Omaha bluffs. Directed by the Spitfires overhead, the massive shells gouged great craters out of the rock and earth particularly at WN-62, killing or stupefying the German defenders.

The first organized attacks made by the Americans came at both ends of Omaha Beach from the shelter of the cliffs. At the western end, soon after 0730 hours men of C/2nd Rangers managed to climb to the top of the cliffs to the west of WN-73, and rather than move at once westward to the Pointe et Raz de la Percée chose to attack eastward, believing at first that they were facing only a small 'fortified house'. Other American troops followed up the cliff, and it took until late afternoon for them to capture the substantial WN-73 position, with 69 Germans dead. At the eastern end of Omaha, L/16th RCT attacked at about 0800 hours using the dead ground. Joined by troops from four other companies including E/116th RCT and aided by accurate shooting from the offshore destroyers, the soldiers fought their way up the Fox-1 la Révolution valley to threaten the coastal highway and to occupy part of WN-60 within the hour.

Meanwhile, American officers and sergeants worked to reorganise their men and gather equipment on the beach. A wounded Col Canham took the western part of 116th RCT landing area, and Brig Gen Cota the eastern

LCI(L) 85, listing heavily, approaches the attack transport *Samuel Chase* to offload its wounded from 1st Medical Battalion's A Company after striking a mine and then being hit by numerous German shells at around 0830 hours. The vessel later capsized and sank at 1430 hours. *(USNA)*

part near les Moulins, moving along the sand, encouraging men and issuing orders. At some point Brig Gen Cota said something to Lt Col Max F. Schneider commanding 5th Rangers that, as later remembered, became the US Rangers' official motto: 'Rangers Lead the Way'. Between 0750 and 0810 hours, engineers using bangalore torpedoes (long tubes filled with explosives) blew a path through the belt of concertina wire, and Brig Gen Cota personally led men of C/116th RCT and 5th Rangers up the bluff between WN-68 and WN-70, moving slowly and carefully in single file because of the landmines and German fire, with other companies to the east joining in the advance. Simultaneously, and aided by direct fire from the surviving Shermans, men of Companies A and B/2nd Rangers worked their up the bluff east of Hamel au Prêtre, before turning to attack WN-70 from the rear. The resistance nest, already heavily damaged by naval shellfire, was taken except for a few Germans who fought on. By 0900 hours, over 600 American troops in

In a photograph that contrasts strongly with those taken by Robert Capa several hours earlier, US reserves (probably from 18th RCT) wade ashore from an LCVP during the late morning of 6 June. Armoured half-tracks towing 57-mm anti-tank guns, and two DUKW amphibious trucks, can also be seen on the beach. *(USNA)*

groups varying from a few men to company strength were on top of the bluff opposite Dog White and moving inland.

While this was happening, another penetration was taking place on the eastern side of les Moulins, between WN-65 and WN-66, with groups of 20–30 American soldiers moving slowly in single file onto the top of the bluff. At 0846 hours, WN-62 reported that the position at WN-67 near St-Laurent was 'probably' in Allied hands, together with WN-65 and WN-66 (both were in fact still held by their garrisons, but under attack). Moving along the top of the bluffs, the Americans were surprised that in many places the German trenches were undefended. Communications between many of the *Widerstandsnester* had failed, and by 1137 hours the first German troops were reported coming out of their bunkers to surrender.

At Easy Red, while naval gunnery and small arms fire kept down the dwindling number of German defenders, gaps were blown in the concertina wire and small parties of soldiers led by Company E/16th RCT moved out from the dead ground between WN-62 and WN-64 to reach the top of the bluff. At 0905 hours German observers reported that WN-61 had fallen, and only one machine gun was still firing from WN-62. Shortly afterwards, and to much astonishment, two German Focke-Wulf Fw 190 fighters made a very low pass along Omaha from the British beaches to the east, flown by *Oberstleutnant* (Lt Col) Josef 'Pips' Priller, a famous *Luftwaffe* ace, and *Feldwebel* (Sergeant) Heinz Wodarczyk, and flew off unharmed. It was the *Luftwaffe*'s only appearance over the Normandy beaches on D-Day.

Turning westward on top of the bluffs, E/16th RCT attacked WN-64 from the rear, capturing it by about 1100 hours and taking 21 prisoners, all who were left of the garrison. About 150 Americans, mainly from G/16th RCT, reached the western edge of Colleville and attacked towards the company command post at WN-63 on the northern side of the village. For the Germans, this small penetration towards Colleville was the most serious event of the day. Shortly before noon, troops of 6/916th Grenadiers were ordered forward from reserve to counter-attack, just before elements of 1/16th RCT got across the coastal road. WN-63 reported that the village had been successfully recaptured, but retaken by the Americans at 1358 hours. Although several small American units fought their way to Colleville and into some of its houses, none record either capturing the village completely or any German counter-attack.

The troops of the next two American infantry regiments to land, 18th Infantry and 115th Infantry, had mostly crossed the Channel in LCI(L)s, each holding a company, in the expectation that the obstacles would be cleared and these big craft could get to the beach. Waiting offshore, 18th Infantry had been set to land starting at 0930 hours at Easy Red, but had suffered the same problems as the first waves of infantry. The attempted landings through the beach obstacles resumed at 1000 hours led by 2/18th Infantry; 28 landing craft were lost in the process, including two LCI(L)s and four LCTs, but most of the men got ashore. Private Carleton W. Barrett of 18th Infantry won the Medal of Honor in this landing by rescuing his comrades under fire in the surf. In an incident many later remembered, at about 1030 hours LCT 30 commanded by Lt Sidney W. Brinker,

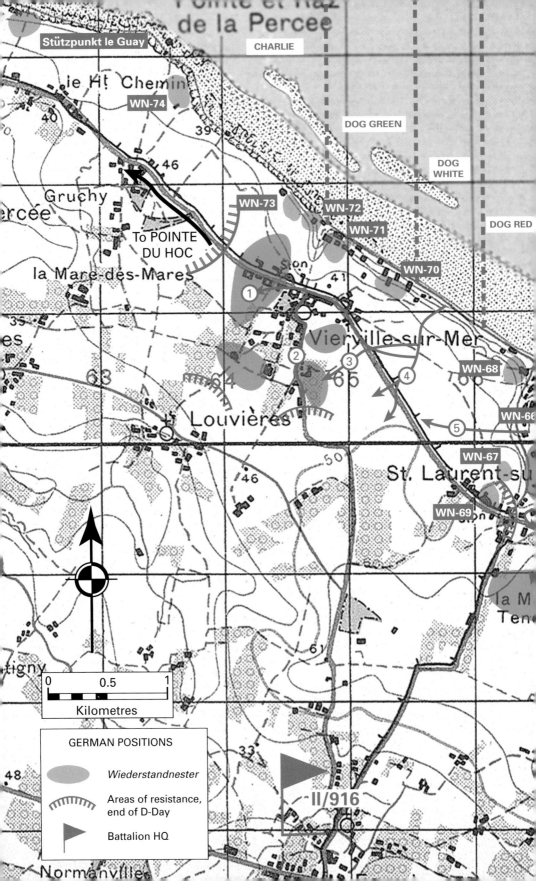

Pointe et Raz
de la Percée

CHARLIE

Stützpunkt le Guay

le Ht Chemin

WN-74

40

DOG GREEN

39

DOG WHITE

46

Gruchy

WN-73

WN-72

DOG RED

To POINTE
DU HOC

WN-71

la Mare-des-Mares

WN-70

41

①

35

②

Vierville-sur-Mer

③

WN-68

64

65

④

Louvières

⑤

WN-66

50

46

WN-67

St. Laurent-su

WN-69

la M
Ten

61

Kilometres

0   0.5   1

GERMAN POSITIONS

Wiederstandnester

Areas of resistance,
end of D-Day

Battalion HQ

II/916

48

33

tigny

Normanville

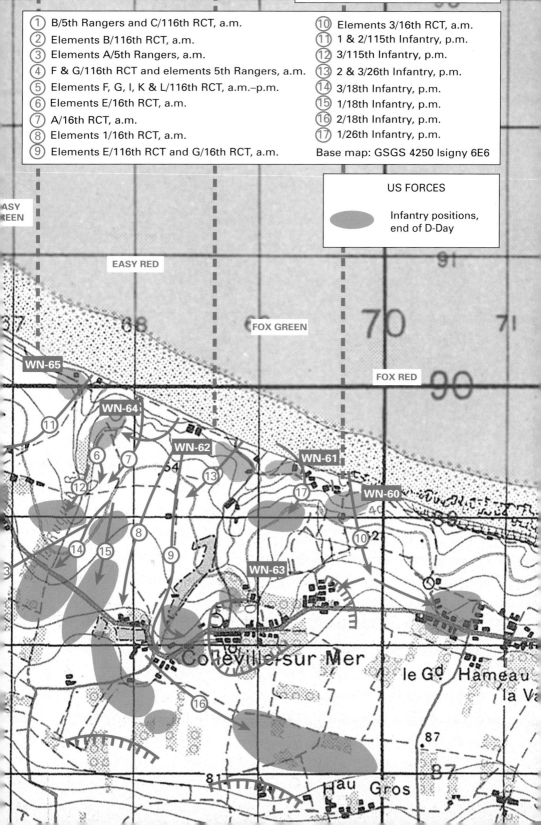

THE ASSAULT, 6 JUNE

① B/5th Rangers and C/116th RCT, a.m.
② Elements B/116th RCT, a.m.
③ Elements A/5th Rangers, a.m.
④ F & G/116th RCT and elements 5th Rangers, a.m.
⑤ Elements F, G, I, K & L/116th RCT, a.m.–p.m.
⑥ Elements E/16th RCT, a.m.
⑦ A/16th RCT, a.m.
⑧ Elements 1/16th RCT, a.m.
⑨ Elements E/116th RCT and G/16th RCT, a.m.

⑩ Elements 3/16th RCT, a.m.
⑪ 1 & 2/115th Infantry, p.m.
⑫ 3/115th Infantry, p.m.
⑬ 2 & 3/26th Infantry, p.m.
⑭ 3/18th Infantry, p.m.
⑮ 1/18th Infantry, p.m.
⑯ 2/18th Infantry, p.m.
⑰ 1/26th Infantry, p.m.

Base map: GSGS 4250 Isigny 6E6

US FORCES

Infantry positions, end of D-Day

EASY GREEN

EASY RED

FOX GREEN

FOX RED

WN-65

WN-64

WN-62

WN-61

WN-60

WN-63

Coleville-sur Mer

le G.d Hameau
la Va

Hau Gros

A view of the Dog-3 exit around noon. The anti-tank ditch which prevented tanks and vehicles moving through the draw can be clearly seen. Some areas show the effects of Allied naval gunfire, but the trench networks of WN-66 (*top left*) and WN-68 (*middle right*) appear to be intact. *(Keele University Air Photo Archive)*

USNR, broke through the obstacles opposite Easy-3 draw and beached, releasing its troops and firing on WN-62 until return fire forced its abandonment; LCI 554 commanded by Lt E.B. Koehler, USNR, beached at the same time and was able to get off after releasing its troops. The reinforcements cheered the Americans and put more pressure on the surviving garrison of WN-62. At 1100 hours the landing craft still milling offshore beyond the obstacles were ordered back to the Line of Departure to reorganise. The tide was starting to turn in both senses, and with the beach getting shallower the big LCIs transferred their troops to smaller craft.

Also by 1100 hours, substantial numbers of American soldiers were off the beach and on top of the bluffs. But few knew where they were, and the advance inland was taking them into the hedgerow country; separate groups were unaware of each other's presence as they moved towards the same objective. More troops of 2/16th RCT penetrated inland as far as Colleville, reinforced by

2/18th Infantry as it moved off the beach at about noon. A small group of 5th Rangers pushed as far as l'Ormel farm (misidentified on American official maps and documents as the Château du Vaumicel, which was a short distance further west), where they were held up by German fire. Troops of 116th RCT including Brig Gen Cota entered Vierville from the east at about 1000 hours, finding the village itself undefended. But attempts to push southwards from the bluffs across the coast road were met with persistently strong German resistance, including a local counter-attack ordered by 5/916th Grenadiers.

On the beach itself at 1100 hours, the shingle bank remained an impassable obstacle to vehicles until it could be cleared by the engineers, and all four draws were still closed and defended. Only the unplanned Fox-1 had been opened, and it had no inland road. The wind and current had raised the incoming tide so much that in places the sea was almost up to the shingle bank, and at least one Sherman on the beach kept firing until the water came over its gun barrel. 1st Lt Jimmy W. Monteith Jr. of 16th Infantry won a Medal of Honor by leading two tanks on foot through a minefield and into positions where they could fire onto the resistance nests, and for then leading his men up the bluffs, before dying further inland. The commander of 743rd Tank Battalion, Lt Col John S. Upham, Jr., was also hit as he tried to lead his men forward on foot. An organised attempt to force Dog-3 draw at 1100 hours after two destroyers had blasted the beach east of les Moulins failed; only three tanks could be assembled, and two of these were destroyed as they tried to advance.

The first of the targeted draws to be opened was Easy-1, aided by E/16th RCT's move westward along the top of the bluffs to capture WN-64, while M/116th RCT pinned down the defenders of the incomplete WN-65. With the draw no longer under observation for German artillery fire, an armoured bulldozer of 37th ECB cleared a path through, earning medals for its two operators. By 1140 hours WN-65 had fallen, and half an hour later the Engineer Special Brigade Group had opened Easy-1 for vehicles. But given

A view of WN-65 at the St-Laurent draw (Easy-1 exit), up the le Ruquet valley, the main exit point for vehicles and heavy equipment on D-Day. The track up the bluff is the one used by American troops after 6 June to advance inland. *(TB)*

the high tide and the state of the beach itself, units continued to land where they could, mainly towards the eastern part of the beach: 115th Infantry, meant to land to the west to reinforce 116th RCT, began coming ashore at 1030 hours almost on top of 2/18th Infantry, while 1/18th Infantry and 3/18th Infantry were delayed until 1300 hours.

Given the situation, 18th Infantry was ordered to take over the planned mission and objectives for 16th Infantry, further intermingling the regiments. It was not until mid-afternoon that 18th Infantry and 115th Infantry had reassembled and begun to move solidly inland. Convoy B2, the fast convoy from Follow-Up Force B, arrived off Omaha at 1530 hours, but was ordered not to start landing until 1630 hours, by which time slow convoy B-3 had joined it in the Transport Area.

With some of the draws being opened and the bluffs being cleared, the ECBs could work clearing lanes through the beach obstacles as the tide receded through the afternoon, although 336th ECB was put ashore at 1500 hours 4,000 metres west of its planned landing area on Fox Green, and had to spend another two hours moving slowly along the length of Omaha under fire. Five large boat channels and six small ones were cleared and marked, mostly on Easy Red leading to Easy-1 and St-Laurent. By 1630 hours, Company B/745th Tank Battalion, the third armoured battalion planned to land on D-Day, was ashore on Fox Green and moving up onto the bluffs, as part of a slow but general American advance off Omaha Beach, reported back to 352nd Infantry Regiment within half an hour by those German resistance nests still in action.

In the wider events of D-Day, the first German impressions of the Omaha landings were that they had failed. At 1140 hours, a report from the Pointe et Raz de la Percée informed 352nd Infantry Division that the beach was covered with American dead and wounded. The much greater threat to 352nd Infantry Division came from British XXX Corps which, after its landing on Gold Beach, had started to push substantially inland. By 0900 hours Battle Group Meyer, halted to the west of Cerisy forest since dawn, was given new orders to turn round, form up north-west of Bayeux, and together with the 10 Sturmgeschütze assault guns of 352nd Anti-tank Battalion to counter-attack this British advance. As part of this return move, at 1030 hours Lt Col Meyer detached II/915th Grenadiers northwards towards Colleville, with the objective of destroying the American penetration inland from Omaha. At the same time, five or six Marder assault guns of 352nd Anti-tank Battalion, together with a company of 352nd Engineer Battalion, were ordered northwards from reserve towards Omaha. Even 352nd Infantry Division's replacement training unit (*Feldersatzbataillon*), some anti-aircraft gunners from 352nd Artillery, and some *Hiwis* and construction unit troops (*Bau-Pi-Einheiten*) were sent to take part. At 1335 hours GenLt Kraiss, commanding 352nd Infantry Division, confidently informed Gen Marcks that, after the defeat of the Americans at Colleville, the beachhead could be considered liquidated. Responsibility for the Pointe du Hoc was transferred to 914th Grenadiers, which despatched a reinforced company of I/914th Grenadiers to eliminate Lt Col Rudder's men.

All these moves were hampered and delayed particularly by the constant harassing presence of Allied fighters and fighter-bombers, which also attacked the vehicles bringing up shells for the German guns; at 1000 hours IV/352nd Artillery reported the ammunition

US Army and Navy medics performed numerous acts of heroism on D-Day. Here, Army medics administer a transfusion to a survivor of a landing craft. (USNA)

supply for its 150-mm howitzers as 'critical'. Because their main reserves were being committed against the other Allied landing beaches, at Omaha the Germans had only infantry companies to send against American battalions and regiments. Throughout D-Day V Corps was never conscious of an organised German counter-attack; instead, the Americans interpreted what were intended as substantial attacks as unexpectedly strong resistance and isolated enemy pockets suddenly appearing in the hedgerow country, occasionally behind them. The attack by the Marders and engineers (certainly ordered and probably attempted) was launched from Formigny towards Vierville in the early afternoon, but was broken up by the guns of USS *Texas* without the Americans ever becoming aware of its nature. The attack by II/915th Grenadiers also seems to have been delayed and broken up by American airpower and naval shellfire, although some of its troops reached the Colleville area by the afternoon, and attempts by 16th RCT to advance eastward from Colleville to the next village of Cabourg were strongly resisted.

At 1223 hours the *Texas* opened fire on WN-71 and WN-72 covering Dog-1 at Vierville, and in response to this shelling the defenders began coming out of their bunkers to surrender. Although German snipers and pockets of resistance continued to fight on, Brig Gen Cota was able to walk downhill along Dog-1 from Vierville to the beach where 121st ECB was starting to clear the draw, and to continue along the beach to Dog-3 at les Moulins. WN-74 and WN-73 continued to fight on until 1625 hours when they signalled their surrender in the face of shellfire from the destroyers offshore. Attempts by 5th Rangers to carry out their main mission by pushing westward along the coast road to the Pointe du Hoc were held up by German machine-gunners firing from the hedgerows, and little progress was made; although by sheer luck one Ranger platoon made it through to join Lt Col Rudder's men at the Pointe du Hoc before nightfall at 2207 hours. The rest of 5th Rangers and 2nd Rangers advanced barely to 800 metres west of Vierville, and 116th RCT only 2,000 metres inland from Dog-1, joined by the remaining tanks of 743rd Tank Battalion, facing troops from III/726th Grenadiers and 352nd Engineer Battalion.

Further to the east, after the first advance up the bluffs, most American formations came inland through or close to Easy-1. For a while, vehicles coming inland from Easy-1, including the remaining tanks of 741st Tank Battalion, were jammed together along the exit road to St-Laurent until engineers cleared other routes. Although troops of 115th Infantry entered St-Laurent by 1600 hours, at nightfall the village was still in German hands and 115th Infantry was barely across the coastal road,

Smoke rising from the entrance to the Dog-1 draw, possibly as the result of the renewed bombardment by the USS *Texas* of German defences in this area. (USNA)

In another famous photograph, taken by US Army Signals Corps photographer Private Louis Weintraub (see p. 105), survivors from a sunk landing craft come ashore on Omaha Beach. (USNA)

while WN-69 to the west controlled the crossroads from Dog-3 at les Moulins. This left a substantial gap in the American position inland between St-Laurent and Vierville, still largely under German fire.

The five artillery battalions planned to land on D-Day came ashore mostly later in the afternoon and evening, having lost 26 guns and much essential equipment between them. At 1615 hours the only Allied field artillery pieces to open fire from Omaha on D-Day, the six surviving 105-mm howitzers of 7th Field Artillery that had begun landing three hours earlier, shelled WN-63 near Colleville. The Germans continued to hold the village as well as the resistance nest, although by 1800 hours 2/18th Infantry had taken up positions 500 metres to the south, surrounding the German garrison from three sides. But the American advance was much delayed in the hedgerows and open ground from Easy-3 draw to St-Laurent and Colleville by unexpected small parties of Germans. These probably included troops of 6/916th Grenadiers making their counter-attack, who GenLt Kraiss believed got as far as recapturing part of WN-65 before being obliterated by offshore gunnery. More troops of II/915th Grenadiers arrived south of Colleville before nightfall, blocking any further American advance southward. At 1940 hours 352nd Infantry Division reported its defensive line at Omaha as running from the edge of Colleville westward through WN-69 and down to the cliffs at WN-74, just inland from the coast road.

By evening the US Navy and Army engineers had opened 13 landing lanes 50–150 metres wide through the beach obstacles. By 2000 hours, 336th ECB had bulldozed an improvised dirt road from Fox-1 to the coast road at Colleville, which could then be used as an exit from the beach for vehicles. At 2100 hours the first troops of 26th Infantry from Follow-Up Force B began to land near Easy-3 and to move inland. Neither Easy-3 itself nor Dog-3 at les Moulins were completely clear of German fire, including shellfire from I/352nd Artillery deep inland, and remained effectively out of use. Dog-1 at Vierville was open by 1800 hours, but concrete debris and German shellfire limited its value. Also among those who came ashore on D-Day was Captain Quentin Roosevelt of 16th Infantry, whose father Brig Gen Theodore Roosevelt Jr. landed on Utah Beach with the first waves.

Among the last units to set up as night fell was the headquarters and Battery A of 320th Barrage Balloon Battalion (VLA) (Colored), with its 'very low altitude' balloons (Battery B of the same battalion landed on Utah Beach on D-Day). Six squadrons of RAF de Havilland Mosquito night fighters took over the defence of the air

A dead GI lies beside a German ramp-type obstacle, on Omaha Beach. *(USNA)*

Concentration etched on his face, an African-American soldier carefully removes shrapnel from the face of a GI on 8 June. *(USNA)*

above the beaches, together with the barrage balloons and anti-aircraft guns. From 2200 hours, the *Luftwaffe* made a series of small raids, including one at Omaha at low level by Junkers Ju 88 medium bombers which narrowly missed the USS *Ancon*; between two and four of the aircraft were shot down. Some aircraft dropped sea mines which continued as a hazard to Allied ships.

Casualty estimates for Omaha Beach on D-Day remain only guesses, for both sides. The chief of staff of 352nd Infantry Division judged later that its casualties were 200 killed, 500 wounded and 500 missing, including troops fighting against the British at Gold Beach. Also some time after the battle, 1st Infantry Division reached a figure of 3,000 Americans killed, wounded and missing, at least 1,000 of them in 116th RCT and 16th RCT, mostly occurring in the first few hours of the landing; 29th Infantry Division gave a precise figure of 341 dead in 116th RCT. By nightfall, 1/116th Infantry had about 250 men able to fight; among the losses for Company A/116th Infantry were 21 of the 34 'Bedford Boys' from the village of Bedford, Virginia, (population 3,000),

including five dead and one wounded from three sets of brothers. Company E of 2/116th Infantry had lost its captain and 104 others, killed, wounded or missing, out of 180; 741st Tank Battalion had only five functioning Sherman tanks remaining from 48 that morning. The US Navy and Royal Navy lost more than 50 landing craft and 10 larger vessels, often with their crews. The Special Engineer Task Force took 52 per cent losses among its Navy personnel, most of them in the first 30 minutes. In Team 1, one of the more successful Gap Assault Teams on D-Day, the 12-man Naval Combat Demolition Unit contingent lost four dead and four wounded.

At 1705 hours Maj Gen Gerhardt, who had arrived with Follow-Up Force B, left the Transport Area for the two hour journey to the shore to establish his 29th Infantry Division's command post. By 1900 hours Maj Gen Huebner had established his 1st Infantry Division command post inland, appropriately code-named 'Danger Forward'. By 2000 hours Maj Gen Gerow had also left for the shore to establish V Corps forward headquarters. His first message to Lt Gen Bradley on USS *Augusta* read simply 'Thank God for the United States Navy!'

CHAPTER 6

SECURING THE BEACHHEAD

For the Allies on D+1 the crisis at Omaha Beach was far from over, and it was by no means certain that the beach would not be abandoned. Having taken prisoners at Omaha from all four infantry regiments of 352nd Infantry Division including 726th Grenadiers, the Americans believed that they were facing the entire division by themselves. Late on D-Day, Montgomery checked with Lt-Gen Dempsey whether US V Corps could be taken through Gold Beach, which was not possible without slowing the British advance. Montgomery, who came ashore on the morning of 8 June, Bradley, who conferred with his corps commanders at Utah and Omaha, and Eisenhower, who viewed the beaches with Admiral Ramsay from the minelayer HMS *Apollo*, all issued the same orders for 7 June : the Allied priority was now to link up the beaches as rapidly as possible.

Omaha Beach was still under German shellfire, and fire from small pockets of riflemen and machine-gunners. At dawn the German launched a local counter-attack that briefly drove Company B, 121st ECB, out of l'Ormel farm. Only about a third of the beach obstacles had been cleared, the exits at Dog-1, Dog-3 and Easy-3 were still not yet properly open, and the landings lagged far behind their scheduled timetables. Out of 3,306 vehicles planned to land on D-Day 2,870 had landed, but of 2,400 tons of supplies barely 100 tons had come ashore; the ammunition situation in particular was critical, and even food was an issue. 745th Tank Battalion had landed overnight and was ready to go into action, but

A grim-faced General Eisenhower watches Allied landing operations from the bridge of HMS *Apollo* on 7 June. *(USNA)*

although infantry and tanks could push into the hedgerows and down the narrow roads, this was country in which a sniper or machine gun could hold up a battalion, and not enough radios were working.

The first priority was to find and destroy the German artillery, and to advance at least as far as the Caen–Cherbourg lateral road to push back any remaining German guns out of range of the beach. As early as 0252 hours USS *Baldwin* silenced one German battery, probably 3/352nd Artillery; HMS *Glasgow* fired on German batteries 13 times during the day, and the big guns of USS *Texas* were in action five times against targets near Formigny and Trévières. Early in the morning, naval gunfire was also brought down briefly on WN-69 west of St-Laurent. Aircraft coming back on patrol over the beach area also joined in with repeated attacks against German positions or moving troops.

After its D-Day losses and achievements, 116th Infantry (no longer part of an RCT) was scarcely capable of resuming the attack; 16th Infantry, 18th Infantry and 115th Infantry were each reinforced by a battalion of 26th Infantry. The third infantry regiment of 29th Infantry Division, 175th Infantry, did not complete its landing until 1630 hours, losing two landing craft to mines, after which the division came back officially under Maj Gen Gerhardt. Although the next division in line, 2nd Infantry Division, began to land on 7–8 June according to timetable, it had to be used at first to hunt down the last remaining Germans near Omaha, and there was a constant awareness that at any time a panzer counter-attack could descend on V Corps' lodgement.

The mayor of Vierville-sur-Mer, Monsieur Leterrier, provides information to an American corporal, 7 June 1944. The two soldiers on the left hold an M1 carbine and a Thompson sub-machine gun respectively. *(USNA)*

According to the original caption, this photograph shows the mayor of Colleville-sur-Mer embracing the first US soldier to enter the village. However, it was probably taken on 7 June, after the Americans secured Colleville. (IWM PL26214)

The German perspective at dawn on 7 June was very different. Some headquarters still believed that the Omaha landings had almost, or even completely, failed. A naval report at 1600 hours on D-Day described the landings as having been wiped out, except for the small remaining pocket on the Pointe du Hoc. Other headquarters were aware of the Allied weakness at Omaha, but for them this was dwarfed in importance by the American achievement at Utah and Ste-Mère-Église, and the Anglo-Canadian successes from Gold all the way to Sword. LXXXIV Corps' first priority remained the defence of Cherbourg, while the panzer divisions as they arrived were put into battle against the British and Canadians around Caen.

At just before midnight on D-Day, GenLt Kraiss advised LXXXIV Corps that the whole of 352nd Infantry Division was committed and had suffered heavy losses, and could maybe hold for another day without reinforcements. In Coast Defence Sector 1, Grandcamp and Maisy had been devastated by Allied bombing and naval bombardment, and 914th Grenadier Regiment was increasingly concerned with the threat to Carentan from the American forces of VII Corps from Utah Beach. To the east in Coast Defence Sector 3, the counter-attack by Battle Group Meyer against the British western flank on D-Day had failed, and 352nd Infantry Division's eastern flank was vulnerable to being rolled up by XXX Corps advancing on Bayeux. The guns of 352nd Artillery were almost out of ammunition and could not be resupplied. For 7 June, as well as getting the 88-mm guns of 1st AA Assault Regiment placed under his command, GenLt Kraiss was given the only remaining reserve available, 30th Mobile Brigade (*Schnelle Brigade 30*), 1,878 men in three infantry battalions on bicycles, which had moved from Coutances in the western Cotentin on D-Day. This brigade lacked heavy weapons and was rated suitable only as a blocking force, but was still ordered to repeat the

counter-attack by Battle Group Meyer against the British, also detaching one battalion, 513th Mobile Battalion, to reinforce 916th Grenadiers at Omaha.

GenLt Kraiss's orders for Coast Defence Sector 2 at Omaha on 7 June were for his troops to attack eastward from the Vierville area and roll up the Americans at least as far as St-Laurent, while holding Colleville as the anvil for the blow. Given their weakness after D-Day, and the increasing power of the American landing, these plans verged on fantasy. In the course of the day, the situation for 352nd Infantry Division became ever more hopeless owing to the rout of 716th Infantry Division on its eastern flank. As Allied analysts later discovered, order and communications within 352nd Infantry Division broke down so completely on 7 June that entirely fictitious German victories were recorded at its headquarters, while units ordered to the Omaha sector had already become scattered, so that their movements and locations cannot be reconstructed with any certainty.

Maj Gen Gerow's plan for V Corps on 7 June was to press on with the D-Day objectives, with 1st Infantry Division driving inland east of a line from St-Laurent to Formigny and 29th Infantry Division west of that line. For 29th Infantry Division, still missing its third infantry regiment and much of its artillery, the priority was clearing the remaining Germans from the beach and the bluffs, and getting help to the Rangers on the Pointe du Hoc. In no condition to make another major attack, 2/116th Infantry and 3/116th Infantry were ordered to clear out the German positions along the bluffs, while four companies of 5th Rangers and some tanks defended Vierville in case the German counter-attack near l'Ormel farm increased in strength. Although no attack by 513th Mobile Battalion materialised during the day, some of its troops may have joined the defenders in that area.

While the two battalions of 116th Infantry moved and fought along the bluffs in the morning, 3/115th Infantry was also ordered to clear St-Laurent and Vierville. Either in the night or under the naval gunnery earlier in the morning

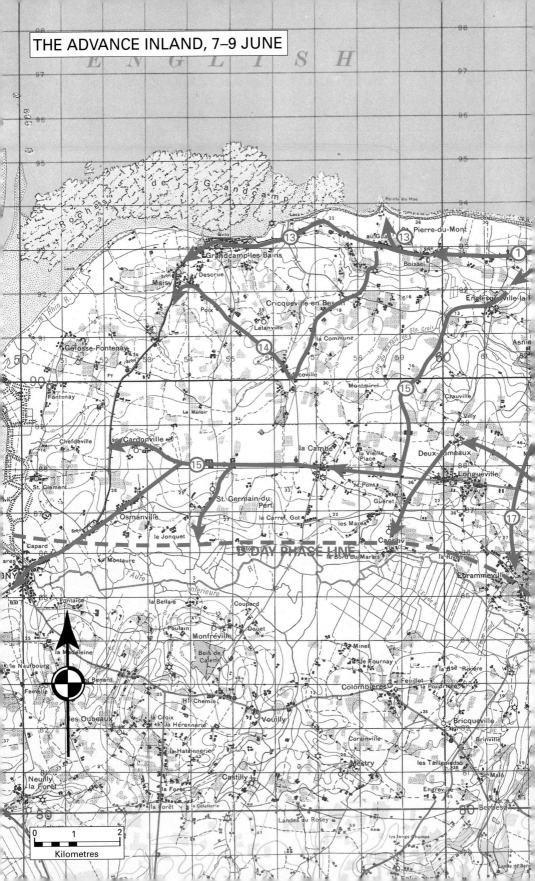

THE ADVANCE INLAND, 7–9 JUNE

① 1/116th Infantry and elements 2nd and 5th Rangers, 7 June
② 1 & 3/115th Infantry, 7 June
③ 2/115th Infantry, 7 June
④ 175th Infantry, 7 June
⑤ 3/26th Infantry, 7 June
⑥ 1/18th Infantry, 7 June
⑦ 3/18th Infantry, 7 June
⑧ 2/26th Infantry, 7 June
⑨ 2/18th Infantry, 7 June
⑩ 1/26th Infantry, 7 June
⑪ 3/16th Infantry, 7 June
⑫ 47 RM Commando, 7–8 June
⑬ 2 & 3/116th Infantry and 2nd and 5th Rangers, 8 June
⑭ 1/116th Infantry, 8 June
⑮ 175th Infantry, 8–9 June
⑯ 3/115th Infantry, 8 June
⑰ 1/115th Infantry, 8 June
⑱ 3/26th Infantry, 8–9 June
⑲ 2/18th Infantry, 8 June
⑳ 2/26th Infantry, 8 June
㉑ 1/26th Infantry, 8 June
㉒ 3/16th Infantry, 8 June
㉓ 2nd Devons, 8 June
㉔ Elements 30 Mobile Brigade and I/726, 8–9 June

Base maps: GSGS 4250 Isigny 6E6, St-Lô 6F2, Creully 7E5, Caen 7F1

WN-69 had been abandoned, and so 3/115th Infantry turned south-west towards the original regimental D-Day objective of the village of Longueville on the northern side of the Lower Aure valley, followed by 1/115th Infantry with 2/115th Infantry joining in later in the day, all these moves encountering German fire. The two battalions of 116th Infantry also took losses when they attempted to push southwards, and at 1700 hours they were pulled back to form a defence for Vierville with the Rangers. At 2000 hours Vierville was shelled by a battery from near Trévières, possibly the 88-mm guns of 3/1st AA Assault Regiment, followed by the expected company-sized infantry attack that was stopped just past l'Ormel farm by American firepower.

Meanwhile, at 0800 hours a force of about 500 men made up from 1/116th Infantry, two companies of 5th Rangers, and the three remaining companies of 2nd Rangers, plus B/743rd Tank Battalion, started a push westward along the coast road towards the Pointe du Hoc, by-passing enemy positions away from the road including the *Stützpunkt* on the Pointe et Raz de la Percée. By 1100 hours they were within 1 km of the Pointe du Hoc position, where Lt Col Rudder's men, backed by fire support from the destroyers, were fighting at close ranges in the hedgerows with troops of I/914th Grenadiers, who were themselves aided by guns of 352nd Artillery and probably also 2/1st AA Assault Regiment. Efforts by the relieving force to get through to Rudder were stopped during the morning by German artillery fire that caused over 30 casualties, but in the afternoon two LCVPs landed supplies and 30 reinforcements at the foot of the cliffs, and patrols reached Rudder's men after nightfall. Next morning, after the remaining companies of 5th Rangers had arrived in support from Omaha, the relief force broke through to the Pointe du Hoc. The casualties in Lt Col Rudder's three companies were 135 men out of 225 who had landed on D-Day.

In 1st Infantry Division's sector, during the night and early morning of 7 June, German troops mainly from 3/726th Grenadiers and 6/916th Grenadiers tried to break out southwards from Colleville and WN-63, only to run into

2/18th Infantry's blocking position to the south; about 50 were killed and 160 captured. By 1000 hours, 2/16th Infantry from the west had cleared the village and the resistance nest, taking another 52 prisoners. It took 1/16th Infantry and 2/16th Infantry the rest of the day to secure the area. The German garrison at Cabourg surrendered early, enabling 3/16th Infantry with B/745th Tank Battalion to drive down the coast road to just short of Port-en-Bessin. Supporting this advance, 62nd Armored Field Artillery with its M7 Priests reported destroying a German medium battery, possibly the four 105-mm guns of 1/352nd Artillery.

In co-ordination with this advance, the main attack from 1st Infantry Division was made to the south-east and south by 18th Infantry with 3/26th Infantry under its command. Moving south-east from Colleville against disorganised German resistance, 2/18th Infantry and some Shermans of C/745th Tank Battalion crossed the River Aure north of the Caen–Cherbourg lateral road, and by 1700 hours had fought their way through to the village of Mosles, just under half-way to Bayeux. Following this up at 1745 hours, 2/26th Infantry continued the advance to the north of the Caen–Cherbourg road through the night.

A little to the west of this advance, 3/18th Infantry crossed the Caen–Cherbourg road at 1700 hours moving southward and by midnight was some 3 km behind the eastern flank of 916th Grenadiers' regimental headquarters at Trévières, close to the original position of 3/1st AA Assault Regiment. A little further west still, 1/18th Infantry advanced southwards, crossing the Caen–Cherbourg road east of Formigny by noon supported by 741st Tank Battalion with its five surviving Shermans, encountering only a few cyclist troops, possibly from 30th Mobile Brigade or

Casualties carried by a converted LCVP wait to be winched on board a larger vessel. The blanket being pulled over the face of one of the men, and the exposed position of the other (despite the poor weather) suggests that help may sadly have arrived too late. *(USNA)*

The devastated German naval radar station at the Pointe et Raz de la Percée, photographed on 22 June 1944. (USNA)

352nd Fusilier Battalion. But Formigny itself remained in German hands; at least some soldiers of II/915th Grenadiers had joined the headquarters of II/916th Grenadiers there, and 3/26th Infantry was unable to dislodge them. Despite the blind nature of the ground, a renewed attack at midnight by Company B of 1/18th Infantry and Shermans of B/745th Tank Battalion against Formigny from the rear and a further attack by 3/26th Infantry next morning captured the village.

Concerned with their own vulnerabilities and the problems of the hedgerow country, the Americans did not realise what their advance to the east and south-east of Omaha on 7 June had achieved. The British had entered Bayeux almost unopposed by midday, cleared the city and pressed on southwards and westwards, and by late afternoon the entire German position north of Bayeux was collapsing, unknown to GenLt Kraiss. Most of the troops of I/726th Grenadiers and 30th Mobile Brigade were being squeezed into a pocket between Bayeux and Port-en-Bessin, and 1st Infantry Division's advance down the Caen–Cherbourg road threatened to trap them all against the coast.

Remarkably, the Germans already knew the American intentions for after D-Day. Late on 6 June a landing craft had drifted ashore in the Vire estuary, from which troops of 914th Grenadiers recovered the plans for VII Corps' advance from Utah Beach. On the evening of 7 June a similar set of plans for V Corps was recovered from the body of an American officer in the fighting south of Vierville. By early on 8 June Rommel had both sets of plans, detailing First US Army's objectives. But although useful, this could not change the German defensive priorities of Cherbourg and the threatened breakout by Second (British) Army, which continued to absorb the German panzer reserves. Omaha Beach was still not a German priority.

In the course of 7 June, despite the random shellfire and snipers, Omaha was transformed from a battleground to a landing and supply area, including starting work on clearing away the shingle barrier from the beach. During the afternoon the first of a series of elderly cargo ships was deliberately sunk off St-Laurent to provide an artificial breakwater code-named Gooseberry, as the start of the 'Mulberry A' harbour to be built there, together with 'Mulberry B' off Arromanches for the British. (The Omaha currents remained treacherous, and work on Mulberry A was abandoned after severe storm damage on 19–22 June.) A further *Luftwaffe* raid at midnight on 7/8 June came close to hitting an important ammunition resupply convoy, and next day the destroyer USS *Meredeth*, part of Task Force O, was sunk by a mine. The landings at Omaha also remained seriously behind schedule; only 1,429 tons of stores were landed that day.

Orders for 29th Infantry Division for 8 June were for 175th Infantry supported by two companies of 747th Tank Battalion to move south-west and then west along the Caen–Cherbourg lateral road, extending all the way through to Isigny the line being taken up by 115th Infantry along the northern side of the Lower Aure valley; while 116th Infantry and 5th Rangers pressed along the coastal road on to Grandcamp and Maisy, where the coastal batteries were still in action. By this time the Germans had

The bridge over the River Aure at Isigny. Although Isigny was devastated by naval bombardment, the bridge itself was captured very early on 9 June by 175th RCT, supported by part of 747th Tank Battalion. *(TB)*

A US 90-mm anti-aircraft gun, operating in the ground support role, assists V Corps' advance inland on 10 June. (USNA)

accepted that their position in the Grandcamp area was hopeless, and troops of 914th Grenadiers together with 439th Ost Battalion were falling back to take part in what would become the defence of Carentan from the west next day. Near the village of Osmanville on the Isigny road after the battle the Americans found two abandoned horse-drawn batteries of 105-mm guns, presumably from II/352nd Artillery. In a solid advance over 36 hours against variable resistance, supported in its last phases by fire from HMS *Glasgow* offshore, by 0300 hours on 9 June the leading Shermans of 747th Tank Battalion entered Isigny, which was already on fire from the naval bombardment. By 0800 the town and its bridge over the River Aure had been secured by 175th Infantry, with over 200 prisoners being taken.

After securing the Pointe du Hoc, 5th Rangers led the advance along the coast road to Grandcamp, with 3/116th Infantry taking over close to the village, which was again heavily shelled by HMS *Glasgow*. Grandcamp, with its complex of bunkers, was captured by nightfall in fighting which some soldiers judged to have been harder than on D-Day itself; another Medal of Honor was won by Technical Sergeant Frank D. Peregory of Company K/116th Infantry. Led by tanks of A/743rd Tank Battalion, 1/116th Infantry cut inland to by-pass Grandcamp to just west of Maisy, and next day German resistance in the area was over.

While this successful advance was happening, 1st Infantry Division began by facing a crisis. In the early hours of 8 June, 18th Infantry headquarters at Surrain received reports of the major German armoured counter-attack that everyone had feared, coming up from the south and overwhelming part of 3/18th Infantry; 1st Infantry Division and V Corps rapidly assembled their armoured reserves, preparing for the worst. It took until 0850 hours to determine that some form of German attack had taken place at about 0200 hours, but not on any scale, and that it had been driven off or destroyed. This diversion was enough to halt 1/18th Infantry and 3/18th Infantry for the day, while 3/115th Infantry dealt with Formigny, and warships including the *Texas* shelled Trévières.

The drive by 26th Infantry to the east, squeezing the side of the German pocket north of Bayeux, was also held up on 8 June to allow the regiment's three battalions to assemble together. At the village of Tour-en-Bessin, 6 km from Bayeux just north of the Caen–Cherbourg road, 2/26th Infantry called in a fighter-bomber strike for the morning and halted; while immediately to the north 1/26th Infantry occupied Etreham, near the high ground at Mont Cauvin, a slope 64 metres high above the River Aure, but encountered strong German resistance along the line of the river itself. Both were waiting for 3/26th Infantry from Formigny, which marched down the Caen–Cherbourg road to join 2/26th Infantry at 1800 hours. Three hours earlier, GenLt Kraiss had regained contact with the commander of I/726th Grenadiers, *Major* Ternieden, trapped with the remaining troops in the pocket, ordering him to fight until nightfall and then break out to the south-west. General Marcks, commanding LXXXIV Corps, confirmed this move, despite the risk of flouting Hitler's orders not to give up ground.

At 2040 hours 3/26th Infantry attacked down the main road towards Bayeux supported by C/745th Tank Battalion, passed through Tour-en-Bessin, and entered into a running fight with the Germans retreating across its front. By 0130 hours next morning 3/26th Infantry had reached its objective at the hamlet of Ste-Anne, only 2 km from the British positions at Vaucelles, the next village along the main road. At Ste-Anne the battalion dug in to face a dark and wild night as, from 0300 hours onwards, the desperate German soldiers and vehicles crashed in the rain around and through their positions, with Allied shellfire bursting all over them. By shortly after dawn the Americans had 125 prisoners, and the pocket was effectively empty.

Above: This view
looks south-
east from Mont
Cauvin, with the
spires of Bayeux
cathedral just
visible towards
the centre of
the horizon.
This critical high
ground
(64 metres) was
secured by US
troops on 8 June.
(TB)

Below: A view of
the port entrance
at Grandcamp-
Maisy. Grandcamp
was captured
before nightfall on
8 June, and later
developed as a
significant entry
point for supplies.
(TB)

On the British side of the pocket, on 8 June No. 47 Royal Marine Commando (battalion) secured Port-en-Bessin, and in the course of the day 50th (Northumbrian) Division from XXX Corps continued its push westward. As night was falling, the westernmost patrol of the commandos met up with troops from Omaha on the coast road, and in the course of the night and next morning 1st Infantry Division established its link with XXX Corps to the east, completing its D-Day objectives. Next day V Corps turned its forces southwards towards St-Lô to begin its new battle. On the evening of 10 June troops from 101st Airborne Division of VII Corps from Utah Beach reached the hamlet of Auville-sur-le-Vey (part of les Veys) just west of the River Vire, making contact with the forward patrols of 175th Infantry (supported by 29th Cavalry Reconnaissance Troop) from Isigny. All the Allied beachheads were at last joined up. 1st Infantry Division estimated its losses from D-Day to D+4 (9 June) as 124 killed, 1,083 wounded, and 431 missing; 29th Infantry Division's estimate was 208 killed, 1,027 wounded, 896 missing; plus a further 148 killed, 656 wounded and 569 missing from other units of V Corps that had fought at Omaha Beach.

PART THREE

BATTLEFIELD TOURS

GENERAL TOURING INFORMATION

Normandy is a thriving holiday area, with some beautiful countryside, excellent beaches and very attractive architecture (particularly in the case of religious buildings). It was also, of course, the scene of heavy fighting in 1944, and this has had a considerable impact on the tourist industry. To make the most of your trip, especially if you intend visiting non-battlefield sites, we strongly recommend you purchase one of the general Normandy guidebooks that are commonly available. These include: *Michelin Green Guide: Normandy*; *Thomas Cook Travellers: Normandy*; *The Rough Guide to Brittany and Normandy*; *Lonely Planet: Normandy*.

TRAVEL REQUIREMENTS

First, make sure you have the proper documentation to enter France as a tourist. Citizens of European Union countries, including Great Britain, should not usually require visas, but will need to carry and show their passports. Others should check with the French Embassy in their own country before travelling. British citizens should also fill in and take Form E111 (available from main post offices), which deals with entitlement to medical treatment, and all should consider taking out comprehensive travel insurance. France is part of the Eurozone, and you should also check exchange rates before travelling.

GETTING THERE

The most direct routes from the UK to Lower Normandy are by ferry from Portsmouth to Ouistreham (near Caen), and from Portsmouth or Poole to Cherbourg. Depending

Page 103: Troops of 2nd Infantry Division (which landed on 7–8 June) scale the bluffs on the west side of the Easy-1 draw, moving inland to support the drive towards St-Lô. The photo was taken from the top of WN-65. *(IWM PL26539)*

on which you choose, and whether you travel by day or night, the crossing takes between four and seven hours. Alternatively, you can sail to Le Havre, Boulogne or Calais and drive the rest of the way. (Travel time from Calais to Caen is about four hours; motorway and bridge tolls may be payable depending on the exact route taken.) Another option is to use the Channel Tunnel. Whichever way you decide to travel, early booking is advised, especially during the summer months.

Although you can of course hire motor vehicles in Normandy, the majority of visitors from the UK or other EU countries will probably take their own. If you do so, you will also need to take: a full driving licence; your vehicle registration document; a certificate of motor insurance valid in France (your insurer will advise on this); spare headlight and indicator bulbs; headlight beam adjusters or tape; a high visibility jacket for use in the event of vehicle breakdown; a warning triangle; and a sticker or number plate identifying which country the vehicle is registered in. Visitors from elsewhere should consult a motoring organisation in their home country for details of the documents and other items they will require.

Normandy's road system is well developed, although there are still a few choke points, especially around the larger towns during rush hour and in the holiday season. As a general guide, in clear conditions it is possible to drive from Cherbourg to Caen in less than two hours.

Several of the US Army Signal Corps photographers whose images appear in this book, pictured on 22 May 1944 in England. From left to right, Private Louis Weintraub; unknown; 1st Lt George Steck; 1st Sgt Val Pope; and Private 1st Class Walter Rosenblum. (USNA)

A statue of a French First World War soldier from the war memorial in Isigny appears to gaze out over the devastated town after its liberation by American forces. This photograph was taken on 8 July 1944. *(USNA)*

ACCOMMODATION

Accommodation in Normandy is plentiful and diverse, from cheap campsites to five star hotels in glorious châteaux. However, early booking is advised if you wish to travel between June and August. Apart from some *gîtes*, there are relatively few places to stay in the immediate vicinity of Omaha Beach. The nearest large town is Bayeux, about 14 km south-east of Colleville-sur-Mer, which offers a good range of hotels to suit all budgets. The coastal resorts of Grandcamp-Maisy and Port-en-Bessin, and the town of Isigny, provide more limited accommodation; telephone or visit their tourist offices for details (*see below*). There are also several campsites in the area, including one at either end of Omaha Beach. Useful contacts include:

French Travel Centre, 178 Piccadilly, London W1J 0AL;
  tel: 0870 830 2000; web: www.raileurope.co.uk
French Tourist Authority, 444 Madison Avenue, New
  York, NY 10022 (other offices in Chicago, Los Angeles
  and Miami); web: www.francetourism.com
Office de Tourisme Intercommunal de Bayeux, Pont
  Saint-Jean, 14400 Bayeux; tel: +33 (0)2 31 51 28 28;
  web: www.bayeux-tourism.com
Calvados Tourisme, 8 Rue Renoir, 14054 Caen;
  tel: +33 (0)2 31 27 90 30;
  web: www.calvados-tourisme.com

Manche Tourisme; web: www.manchetourisme.com

Maison du Tourisme de Cherbourg et du Haut-Cotentin,
  2 Quai Alexandre III, 50100 Cherbourg-Octeville;
  tel: +33 (0)2 33 93 52 02;
  web: www.ot-cherbourg-cotentin.fr

Office de Tourisme Grandcamp-Maisy, 118 Rue
  A-Briand; tel: +33 (0)2 31 22 62 44.

Office de Tourisme Port-en-Bessin, 2 Rue du Croiseur-
  Montcalm; tel: +33 (0)2 31 21 92 33.

Office de Tourisme Isigny-sur-Mer, 1 Rue Victor Hugo,
  BP 110; tel: +33 (0)2 31 21 46 00.

Gîtes de France, La Maison des Gîtes de France et du
  Tourisme Vert, 59 Rue Saint-Lazare, 75 439 Paris
  Cedex 09; tel: +33 (0)1 49 70 75 75;
  web: www.gites-de-france.fr

In addition to those listed, there are tourist offices in all the large towns and many of the small ones, especially along the coast.

BATTLEFIELD TOURING

Each volume in this series contains from four to six battlefield tours. These are intended to last from a few hours to a full day apiece. Some are best undertaken using motor transport, others should be done on foot, and many involve a mixture of the two. Owing to its excellent infrastructure and relatively gentle topography, Normandy also makes a good location for a cycling holiday; indeed, some of our tours are ideally suited to this method.

In every case the tour author has visited the area concerned before the original edition of this book was published, in 2004. Since then, land use, infrastructure annd rights of way have altered in some areas, although this is not necessarily reflected in current French mapping. With care, however, it should not be too difficult to identify those small changes that have occurred and to amend one's route accordingly. If you encounter difficulties in following any tour, we would very much like to hear about it, so we can incorporate changes in future editions. Your comments should be sent to the publisher at the address provided at the front of this book.

To derive maximum value and enjoyment from the tours, we suggest you equip yourself with the following items:

- Appropriate maps. European road atlases can be purchased from a wide range of locations outside France. However, for navigation within Normandy, the French Institut Géographique National (IGN) produces maps at a variety of scales (www.ign. fr). The 1:100,000 series ('Top 100') is particularly useful when driving over larger distances; sheet 06 (Caen – Cherbourg) covers most of the invasion area. For pinpointing locations precisely, the current IGN 1:25,000 Série Bleue is best. Extracts from map editions available in 2004 were used for the tour maps in this series, although in a few cases newer editions have appeared since then. These maps can be purchased in many places across Normandy and from specialist dealers in the UK (e.g. www.themapcentre.com or www.stanfords.co.uk). Allow at least a fortnight's notice, as maps are not always in stock.
- Lightweight waterproof clothing and robust footwear are essential, especially for touring in the countryside.
- Take a compass, provided you know how to use one!
- A camera and spare memory cards.
- A notebook to record what you have photographed.
- A French dictionary and/or phrasebook. (English is widely spoken in the coastal area, but is much less common inland.)
- Food and drink. Although you are never very far in Normandy from a shop, restaurant or *tabac*, many of the tours do not pass directly by such facilities. It is therefore sensible to take some light refreshment with you.
- Binoculars. Most officers and some other ranks carried binoculars in 1944. Taking a pair adds a surprising amount of verisimilitude to the touring experience.

SOME DOS AND DON'TS

Battlefield touring can be an extremely interesting and even emotional experience, especially if you have read something about the battles beforehand. In addition, it is fair to say that residents of Normandy are used to visitors, among them battlefield tourers, and generally will do their best to help if you encounter problems. However, many of the tours in the 'Battle Zone Normandy' series are off the beaten track, and you can expect some puzzled looks from the locals, especially inland. In all cases we have tried to ensure that tours are on public land, or viewable from public rights of way. However, in the unlikely event that you are asked to leave a site, do so immediately and by the most direct route.

In addition: **Never remove 'souvenirs' from the battlefields.** Even today it is not unknown for farmers to turn up relics of the 1944 fighting. Taking these without permission may not only be illegal, but can be extremely dangerous. It also ruins the site for genuine battlefield archaeologists. Anyone returning from France should also

Private Alfonton Ortega of Los Angeles paints some of the crosses used in the first American cemetery established at Omaha Beach soon after D-Day. *(USNA)*

One of the *Comité du Débarquement* monuments found throughout Normandy. This russet-coloured stone monument to the Allied landings on Omaha Beach stands on the seafront at les Moulins, on the boundary of Dog Red and Easy Green. *(TB)*

remember customs regulations on the import of weapons and ammunition of any kind.

Be especially careful when investigating fortifications. Some of the more frequently-visited sites are well preserved, and several of them have excellent museums. However, both along the coast and inland there are numerous positions that have been left to decay, and which carry risks for the unwary. In particular, remember that many of these places were the scenes of heavy fighting or subsequent demolitions, which may have caused severe (and sometimes invisible) structural damage. Coastal erosion has also undermined the foundations of a number of shoreline defences. Under no circumstances should underground bunkers, chambers and tunnels be entered, and care should always be taken when examining above-ground structures. If in any doubt, stay away.

Beware of hunting (shooting) areas (signposted *Chasse Gardée*). Do not enter these, even if they offer a short cut to your destination. Similarly, Normandy contains a number of restricted areas (military facilities and wildlife reserves), which should be avoided. Watch out, too, for temporary footpath closures, especially along sections of coastal cliffs.

If using a motor vehicle, keep your eyes on the road. There are many places to park, even on minor routes, and it is always better to turn round and retrace your path than to cause an accident. In rural areas avoid blocking entrances and driving along farm tracks; again, it is better to walk a few hundred metres than to cause damage and offence.

THINGS TO DO IN THE OMAHA BEACH AREA

Thanks to its expanse of golden sand and reasonably good facilities, Omaha Beach is a popular destination for family groups, especially during the summer. Walkers and cyclists will also find the area appealing; there are several well marked routes through attractive scenery along the coast and further inland. Check with the local tourist offices about the status of the clifftop path between Omaha Beach and Grandcamp-Maisy, however, before exploring this particular route.

To the east there are several interesting and appealing small coastal towns within easy reach, among them Port-en-Bessin and Arromanches-les-Bains, both of which offer excellent cuisine and sites of historical interest. To the west of Omaha Beach, Grandcamp-Maisy has a marina and some good restaurants, while Isigny is a centre of the dairy industry, with associated farm produce in abundance.

The 29th Infantry Division memorial, looking up Dog-1 draw towards Vierville-sur-Mer. (DN)

Any visitor wishing to take a day off from battlefield touring would be well advised to explore the fascinating and beautiful town of Bayeux. As well as the famous Bayeux Tapestry museum there are streets of charming and interesting buildings to walk through, and some excellent shopping. The cathedral is of considerable architectural merit, and there are plenty of cafés and restaurants for those who wish simply to sit and relax. Bayeux is also the location for the superb Battle of Normandy Museum, containing numerous exhibits covering the entire Battle of Normandy. It makes an obvious starting point for any battlefield tour within the Calvados département. The largest Commonwealth War Graves Commission military cemetery in Normandy, with 3,935 British and 813 other war graves, is almost directly opposite the museum.

Another place worth a short visit is Formigny, a few kilometres south of St-Laurent-sur-Mer. It was here in 1450 that a battle was fought between the French and English,

BATTLE OF NORMANDY MUSEUM

Musée Mémorial de la Bataille de Normandie, Boulevard Fabian Ware, 14400 Bayeux; tel: +33 (0)2 31 51 46 90; email: <bataillenormandie@mairie-bayeux.fr>. Open 0930–1830 daily 1 May–30 Sept, otherwise 1000–1230 & 1400–1800 daily, closed for two weeks in Jan. Entrance fee.

which saw the latter driven out of Normandy. The Chapelle St-Louis in the village was built to commemorate the battle and contains a number of relics from it. Some 14 km further south, astride the main road between Bayeux and St-Lô (D 572), is the Forêt de Cerisy nature reserve, with various walks and picnic areas. On the western edge of the forest is the village of Cerisy-la-Forêt, the location of a great Benedictine abbey, partly ruined. On the opposite side of the woodland you will find the town of Balleroy, with its impressive château (+33 (0)2 31 21 60 61); there is a hot air balloon museum at the same location. Other tourist sites (for example Caen and Mont-St-Michel) are within an hour or two's drive of the Omaha Beach area.

THE OMAHA BEACH TOURS

This section of the book contains four tours, focusing on the experience of US V Corps on D-Day itself. Each is illustrated with an extract from the current IGN 1:25000 scale Série Bleue map sheet (1412 OT, 'Pointe du Hoc, Omaha Beach'). Together, these extracts cover most of the D-Day assault area, but not the coast between Vierville and the Pointe du Hoc. If you wish to visits the sites of the other actions described in this book, the IGN map mentioned above will be invaluable.

To discover more about the fighting on either flank of Omaha Beach, consult *Gold Beach* and *Utah Beach* in this series. To find out about the battles fought by US V Corps from 9 June onwards, see also *Battle for St-Lô* in the series.

POINTE DU HOC

OBJECTIVE: This tour covers the assault by Companies D, E and F, 2nd Rangers, against the 2nd Battery, 1260th Coastal Artillery Detachment, on Pointe du Hoc.

DURATION/SUITABILITY: The tour lasts two to three hours. The total distance covered is small; the Pointe du Hoc site, managed by the American Battle Monuments Commission, covers only 30 acres. The route to Stand A5 is about 2.5 km, round trip. The small area involved and the rugged nature of the terrain mean that all stands are reached on foot. Those with mobility difficulties can access Stand A2 with few problems, but reaching the others may be harder. The best approach would be to negotiate the route as far as possible across the few tarmac paths, or in dry conditions across level ground, and safely attain vantage points that give a view of the areas under discussion.

STARTING THE TOUR: The most likely approach is along the D514 coast road. There is a roundabout at the entrance to the Pointe du Hoc site, which provides access to a vehicle park constructed for the 60th anniversary of D-Day commemorations in 2004. This car and coach park covers a large area, and is not shown on the map overleaf (it occupies the area where the telephone symbol appears on that map, as well as several fields north-east of 'le Bavent'; the approach road from the D514 has also been widened and straightened and the original car park grassed over). Park here and walk towards the north-western corner of the car park (not the eastern end, through which most visitors enter), where there is an entrance to the site.

① LCA 861, E Coy
② LCA 862, E Coy
③ LCA 888, Lt Col Rudder & E Coy
④ LCA 722, E Coy
⑤ LCA 668, D Coy
⑥ LCA 858, D Coy
⑦ LCA 887, F Coy
⑧ LCA 884, F Coy
⑨ LCA 883, F Coy
⑩ Casemate No. 4
⑪ Casemate No. 5
⑫ Emplacement No. 6
⑬ 20-mm AA position
⑭ Advance by elements D & E Coys, 0715-0815 hours
⑮ Advance by elements F Coy, 0715-0815 hours
⑯ German counter-attacks, afternoon 6 June
⑰ Approximate location of five 155-mm guns
⑱ Forward positions, 2nd Rangers, evening 6 June
⑲ German counter-attacks, night 6-7 June
a Ranger Road

Base map: IGN 1412OT

Pointe du Hoc

le Bavent

D 5 1 4

To
GRANDCAMP-
MAISY

le Guay

la Montagne

l'Église

Manoir
de St-Pierre

VIERVILLE-SUR-M[

de St-P[

D514

0   250   5[
Metres

Right: The needle of rock at the apex of the Pointe du Hoc. *LCA 861*, carrying men of E Company, 2nd Rangers, led by Lt Lapres, grounded near this area. *(SCT)*

STAND A1: THE CLIFF ASSAULT

DIRECTIONS: Near the entrance to the site is a 155-mm gun barrel mounted on a concrete and steel rest. This gun is similar to the six captured French guns that were assigned to the position. Continue past the gun along 'James E. Rudder Path' to the apex of the position. This is marked by the Ranger Memorial, shaped like a dagger from roughly hewn stone. During the walk it will probably prove impossible not to linger and gaze at the overwhelming image of devastation confronting you. The best vantage point is Casemate 4, which has a viewing platform.

At the Ranger Memorial join the track running east along the cliff for just over 200 metres until you reach a substantial concrete structure, with a metal walkway around it, that stands right on the cliff edge. This structure mounted a 20-mm anti-aircraft gun on 6 June 1944. During the battle it became the command post of Lt Col Rudder, who led the assault. The command post lies roughly at the centre of the sector of cliffs assaulted by Rudder's men. Looking west to the Ranger Memorial there are good views of the cliff with its needle of rock in front. It also provides a graphic illustration of the daunting task the Rangers faced. On the cliff top approximately 400 metres to the east there was a machine-gun nest covering the beach and area immediately inland.

Below: Casemate 4, with the viewing position on top. This is an excellent place from which to gain a panoramic view of the whole Pointe and the awe-inspiring level of destruction inflicted by Allied air and naval attacks. *(SCT)*

THE ACTION: The Provisional Ranger Force had three sequential objectives on D-Day. First, capture the Pointe and destroy the German coastal battery. Second, advance inland to secure and hold the coast road (now the D514) until the arrival of 116th RCT from Omaha. Third, push rapidly westward along the coast road through Grandcamp and Maisy towards Isigny-sur-Mer, 12 km from the Pointe, by nightfall.

Lt Col Rudder's plan for achieving the first, critical, objective was an initial assault by Ranger Force A, drawn from elements of 2nd Rangers. Preceded by an air and naval bombardment, E and F Companies, with a headquarters detachment, were to attack the eastern side of the Pointe, D Company the western. H-Hour was 0630. A and B Companies, 2nd Rangers, and 5th Rangers were to await the success signal before landing. If the assault failed, or no signal was received after 30 minutes, these units were to join C Company, 2nd Rangers, at Vierville-sur-Mer on Omaha Beach, and proceed to the Pointe.

In the early morning of 6 June, the 225 men of Ranger Force A were embarked in 10 LCAs, accompanied by two supply craft and four DUKW amphibians. However, *LCA 860* and a valuable supply craft were both swamped by heavy seas. A navigation error by the guide vessel carried the force eastward, away from the objective, before the mistake was corrected. As the Americans approached from the east, over 30 minutes late, sporadic fire from the cliffs indicated that the defences were recovering from the effects of the pre-H-Hour aerial and naval bombardment. Rather than risk the further delay required if D Company were to sweep round to the western side of the Pointe, Rudder ordered it to land with the other two. At 0708 hours, 38 minutes after H-Hour, nine LCAs hit the beaches at the foot of the eastern side of the Pointe du Hoc under covering fire from HMS *Talybont*.

As the Rangers landed, they came under attack from German troops using small arms and grenades from the cliff tops. The most sustained fire was from the machine-gun position on the cliff to the east that enfiladed much of the beach itself. Rangers in *LCA 861* approaching the base of the Pointe drove a small group of Germans back from the cliff edge with their fire. Near the eastern end of the line of craft, *LCA 884* suffered only three casualties from the machine gun by using a powerful combination of its own Lewis light machine guns and Browning Automatic Rifles (BARs) to suppress the position.

Further problems in disembarking were caused by terrain. *LCA 861, 888, 668* and *887* grounded short of the beach on debris blasted into the sea. D Company men on *LCA 668* were forced to swim the last few metres to shore under fire. 1st Sgt Leonard G. Lomell was wounded, but managed to get ashore with his equipment for climbing the cliff. Allied fire had also gouged the shingle beach with deep craters filled with water and mud. *LCA 858, 887* and *884* were unable to avoid lowering their ramps on the edge of these features. Stepping off *LCA 884*'s ramp, Lt Jacob J. Hill's team from F Company plunged in to shoulder-high water. Heavily laden, they struggled to get out of the crater, though all eventually succeeded. Moving across the beach, zig-zagging to avoid German fire and more craters, the Rangers swiftly gathered under cover at the base of the cliff. German fire dramatically reduced when the destroyer USS *Satterlee* opened fire at German troops observed on the Pointe.

The Rangers quickly organised to climb the cliff. On landing, each LCA had fired three pairs of rocket-propelled grappling irons, attached to ropes and rope ladders, to enable a rapid ascent. Success varied greatly. None of *LCA 861*'s grapnels reached the cliff top, whilst *LCA 883*, firing from very close in, secured five lines. Some lines were waterlogged and failed to carry. On the beach, Rangers used hand-projector rockets, again with mixed success. Technical Sgt John I. Cripps fired four rockets; each time he was momentarily blinded and showered in dirt. Scaling the lines that seemed to be secure also proved to be difficult. Private Harry W. Roberts fell back to the beach after his first line came loose, or was cut by the Germans. In places, lack of footholds and poor grip on slippery ropes made the ascent difficult and tiring. Light steel ladders were also used to reach the German positions above the beach but plans

From Rudder's
command
post, looking
west. The view
through the
barbed wire
gives a good
idea of what the
Germans could
see during the
first stages of the
Rangers' attack.
(TB)

to use 30-metre extendable fire engine ladders mounted on DUKWs failed when beach craters prevented them driving to the base of the cliff.

Light opposition meant that the Rangers suffered few casualties in the ascent. By around 0745 hours, just over 30 minutes after landing, most of the Rangers had reached the top. The code message 'Praise the Lord' (meaning 'all men on the cliff') was transmitted, but no reply was received. Unfortunately, Ranger Force A was now isolated. At 0710 hours, having failed to receive the signal that the assault had succeeded, the remainder of the Provisional Ranger Force had proceeded to Omaha.

STAND A2: ASSAULT ON THE POINTE

DIRECTIONS: Walk back along the track to the Ranger Memorial. This stands on top of the German observation bunker responsible for directing the fire of the heavy guns. Sadly, risk that these features may collapse because of coastal erosion has led the authorities to place barbed wire to prevent access. To the east lies the cliff over which the Rangers emerged on to the Pointe. Turn to face towards the car park and study the terrain over which they had to move. Note the two, relatively intact, gun casemates, Nos. 4 and 5, some 80 and 200 metres away.

THE ACTION: Each company had been given specific objectives for the attack against the main positions on the Pointe. E Company was assigned the observation post and gun emplacement 3 sited immediately in front of the cliff face. Immediately east, F Company was to secure emplacements 1 and 2. D Company's targets were casemates 4 and 5 and emplacement 6, facing the western side of the Pointe. When these tasks were completed the companies were to assemble at the southern edge of the position (near the present-day road entrance to the car park) before advancing to the coast road.

The Rangers reached the top of the cliffs in scattered groups. Trained to move with speed, they did not wait to form up into squads or platoons, but immediately moved off to carry out their missions. The scene of devastation that greeted them, bearing none of the expected landmarks, caused the Rangers some trouble in identifying their objectives. Groups became separated while crossing the broken terrain and were usually unaware of the presence of others nearby intent on their own advance. At the gun positions, the Rangers found that the emplacements were heavily damaged, and the guns had been withdrawn.

1st Sergeant Leonard G. Lomell recalled the attack on the artillery positions:

'My platoon couldn't wait for nothing: we had our assignment, and we in Company D depended on a lot of speed. My second platoon went ahead in a rush. We had some confrontations coming out of shell craters, and one of my sergeants, Morris Webb,

The remains of a steel-reinforced bunker near the cliff top give a dramatic demonstration of the effects of the bombardment. The USS *Texas* saturated the Pointe with fire from its ten 14-inch guns prior to the Rangers' landing. *(DN)*

The cliff-top headquarters of Lt Col Rudder's Provisional Ranger Force. The Stars and Stripes draped over the rocky outcrop was placed to prevent Allied warships firing at the Rangers. (USNA)

as we were charging out of a shell crater, a machine gun opened up, and he jumped back into the crater right on top of one of his men's bayonet that went right through his side.

We didn't stop: we played it just like a football game, charging hard and low. We went into the shell craters for protection, because there were snipers around and machine guns firing at us, we'd wait for a moment, and if the fire lifted, we were out of that crater and into the next one. We ran as fast as we could over to the gun positions – to the one that we were assigned to. There were no guns in the positions!'

Source: Personal account on 'American Experience of D-Day' website: www.pbs.org/wgbh/amex/dday/sfeature

The only significant resistance along the cliff edge was around the observation point (OP). Finding themselves on the cliff directly in front of the OP, Staff Sgt Charles H. Denbo and Private Roberts came under fire as they tried to reach the cover of a nearby trench. Successfully throwing three grenades through the firing slits they silenced the machine gun, although Denbo was wounded by rifle fire. Minutes later the second of two bazooka rounds exploded inside the observation post, fired by Sgt Andrew J. Yardley, who had reached the trench with Lt Theodore E. Lapres and two other Rangers. Lapres then took some of the Rangers round the western side of the OP to its rear.

The appearance of Lapres and his men came as a surprise to Corporal Victor J. Aguzzi, who was lying in a crater at the rear of the OP covering the entrance. He had been part of a five-man team led by Lt Joseph E. Leagans that had approached the OP from the east, forcing a German throwing grenades over the cliff to retire inside. Noting that the OP's aerial had been shot away, Leagans decided to leave Aguzzi to cover the entrance until demolition squads arrived. Leagans and the rest of the group pushed forwards. Lapres and some of his men also moved on.

Soon after, Sgt Yardley was joined by four more Rangers, from *LCA 861*, whose arrival prompted a new burst of fire from the OP. Yardley then hit the bunker with another bazooka round and three of the men moved along the trench to the west side of the OP. Dashing across open ground, two of them passed Aguzzi but the other was killed. All this time the Americans on either side of the OP were oblivious to each others' presence.

On the cliff east of Rudder's command post, attempts to reduce the German machine-gun post also proved frustrating. Some time in the morning it was finally silenced when the section of cliff that the gun stood on was blown into the sea by naval gunfire. Before this, men from F Company had made three vain attempts to take the position.

Above: A view of the remains of the 20-mm anti-aircraft position along the eastern side of the cliffs that became Lt Col Rudder's command post during the fighting on the Pointe on 6–8 June. This is the same position as in the photo on p.120 *(TB)*

Opposite: View through the embrasure of the German 20-mm anti-aircraft position on the western side of the Pointe. The ground around the 155-mm mounted gun barrel visible in the middle distance on the right was the area for one of the German counter-attacks on 6 June. *(TB)*

Some confusion exists as to which ship fired the salvo. Throughout the morning, and into mid-afternoon radio problems forced the Rangers to rely upon Lt James W. Eikner using a signal lamp to relay fire requests to the destroyers. Stephen Ambrose argues that Lt Eikner signalled the USS *Satterlee* for the decisive rounds but official accounts claim that Lt Johnson, 58th Armored Field Artillery Battalion, attached to the Rangers, directed fire from HMS *Talybont*.

STAND A3:
THE GERMAN ANTI-AIRCRAFT POSITION

DIRECTIONS: Walk back to the main path and go towards the car park. Pass the casemate with the viewing stand and continue to the second. Look towards the western cliff edge. About five metres in from the cliff you should see a low, intact concrete structure, another 20-mm anti-aircraft gun position. Walk half way to it. To the rear are trees running to the car park. In 1944 a lane ran along here through open ground strewn with mines and barbed wire, to join the exit road from the Pointe in what is now the car park. Face back in the direction of the 155-mm gun.

Those with mobility difficulties should note that, although there are no paths leading to this stand, the ground here is flat and fairly easily negotiated. Alternatively, if conditions are unfavourable, it is best to take up a position near emplacement 6 from which it is possible to see the salient features.

THE ACTION: Lt Col Rudder moved his headquarters to the 20-mm anti-aircraft position atop the eastern cliff at around 0745 hours. This came under sniper fire from the area of casemate 4 (today's viewing platform). Two

Rangers sent to deal with the threat soon found themselves ordered to silence a machine gun firing from the 20-mm anti-aircraft position on the western cliff edge. *En route* they stumbled across a party of around ten Rangers in cover near emplacement 6. Whilst moving cautiously towards the gun the group was suddenly dispersed by mortar and artillery fire, when one of the Rangers gave away their location by firing at a German helmet raised above a crater on a stick. Only Private William Cruz managed to return to the American command post; most of the others appear to have been taken prisoner. During his perilous return he had heard German machine-pistol fire amongst the craters, indicating either that fresh German troops had infiltrated on to the Pointe, or that the garrison was emerging from its bunkers.

Rudder, wounded in the thigh, was now left with an uncomfortable predicament. It was possible that a counter-attack launched from the western part of the Pointe might regain the cliffs. This would leave the rest of his force isolated as they advanced inland. To secure the cliffs, Captain Otto Masny was instructed to round up remaining elements of his F Company, headquarters staff, wounded, and any other personnel, to form a defensive perimeter around the command post.

Above: Damage from naval gunfire can still be seen on the walls of casemate 5, though it is clearly still capable of operating had any gun been deployed inside (see *photo on p.124 for how it looked in 1944*). Only two covered casemates for the 155-mm guns deployed on the Pointe had been completed by 6 June. *(TB)*

A GI looks at casemate 5 on Pointe du Hoc. This photo was taken after Rudder's men had been relieved on 8 June by elements from 116th RCT and 5th Rangers, supported by 743rd Tank Battalion. *(USNA)*

While carrying out these orders under fire, Masny decided to attack the German anti-aircraft position west of the Pointe. Moving across the broken ground with eight Rangers, he headed south-west from the command post towards the exit road. On the way the group picked up several scattered contingents. About 130 metres south-east of casemate 5, the group turned west along a lane that ran behind the German gun position (in the trees to the rear of the stand). After some 80 metres they were engaged by small arms, machine-gun and mortar fire to their left and from the 20-mm emplacement. After a short but fierce fire-fight, accurate artillery fire smashed the group, killing four and wounding the rest.

Realising the futility of his position Masny ordered the survivors to withdraw. Retreating toward the command post, Masny and a private were pursued by a sniper. When Masny ran out of ammunition for his sub-machine gun, they destroyed the radio with the last two rounds in the private's pistol, and sought cover in a crater. Luckily, they stumbled across Staff Sgt James E. Fulton resting from the morning's labours. Raising his helmet on the barrel of his gun Masny drew the sniper's attention, then Fulton killed him, firing a full magazine of 20 rounds from his BAR.

Overall the two abortive attacks had cost the Rangers 15–20 casualties.

STAND A4:
THE GERMAN COUNTER-ATTACKS

DIRECTIONS: Return to the Ranger Memorial and walk back along the cliff edge towards Rudder's command post. About 100 metres along are the remains of emplacement 3 with its distinctive round concrete base. From here, first look towards the woods south-east of Rudder's CP. This was open ground in 1944, across which the Germans launched attacks from St-Pierre-du-Mont. Another counter-attack came from the direction of what is now the car park towards Rudder's CP.

THE ACTION: Initial German reaction to the attack had been tentative. The headquarters of 352nd Infantry Division received the news around 0805 hours, but sent only one platoon of 9th Company, 726th Grenadiers, based at Englesqueville, to counter-attack. Shortly after, a report that Allied troops had scaled the cliff was the last information the division had until 1110 hours. By this time all German reserves had been committed. However, local commanders probably also drew on construction and support units in the area. Additionally, throughout the battle the Rangers noted the Germans had considerable fire support, possibly from 2/352nd Artillery (105-mm guns), two German batteries at Maisy (155-mm and 105-mm guns) and II/1st Anti-Aircraft Assault Regiment (88-mm guns).

The first attack in the afternoon came against the Rangers' eastern flank. There was an hour-long fire-fight, with the Germans setting up a machine gun in a hedgerow south of the Rangers' position. Though supported by artillery, the fall of shot was poor, with most of the rounds passing over the cliffs into the sea. Even so the Rangers faced a difficult time. The Germans were too close to use naval guns against them and, with little ammunition for their single 60-mm mortar, the Rangers were forced to husband its fire.

At 1600 hours there was a much stronger and better co-ordinated thrust against the western flank in front of

Above: View south-west from near the Pointe, showing (*top right*) the 20-mm anti-aircraft position beside the cliff that formed one of the central points of German resistance, and a base from which counter-attacks were organised against the Rangers' positions. *(TB)*

the Ranger CP. Two groups of Germans managed to get close to the Rangers' positions. One group, approaching from the 20-mm position on the west cliff, was spotted by Staff Sgt Herman E. Stein. A close range burst from his BAR killed several and startled the others into withdrawing. The other group was initially thrown into confusion by mortar fire. This delay enabled the Rangers to reinforce the western flank. The Germans fired against this section of the line, but the only effect was to assist the Rangers in spotting targets for their mortar's remaining ammunition. The Germans were forced in to a hasty withdrawal and the immediate threat to the cliff position receded.

STAND A5: THE GERMAN GUNS

DIRECTIONS: This stand is situated in a quiet country lane 1.5 km south of the Pointe du Hoc. It may be possible to reach it on foot using the route shown on the tour map, although in recent years vegetation has blocked the northern entrance to the lane to the extent that it has become almost inaccessible. It may be easier, therefore, to drive to the southern entrance of the lane near la Montagne (adjacent to the buildings shown at Point 21 near the bottom left-hand corner of the map on p. 114). There is room to park a car on the verge here before approaching stand A5 on foot from the south.

THE ACTION: Small groups of Rangers advanced along this route on 6 June towards the coastal road. They found a roadblock halfway down, and were constantly harassed by sniper fire. About 30 Rangers from D and E Companies reached the main road at 0815 hours. This force soon increased to 50 when men from F Company arrived. They had advanced through the fields east of the road, and then the village of le Guay (Au Guay on Allied maps in 1944), meeting light resistance *en route*.

The Rangers now deployed into the fields south of the coastal road. At the southern end of three fields they found German trenches dug into the north side of the hedgerows running along them. Elements of D Company took up position just beyond the junction with a sunken lane to the west. From these positions the Rangers could cover the road and the valley to the south, blocking any German attempts to reach the road and the Pointe from these directions. During a patrol down the sunken lane, 1st Sgt Lomell and Staff Sgt Jack E. Kuhn came across the German guns camouflaged in a field to the west.

1st Sergeant Leonard G. Lomell described destroying the guns:

'I said, "Jack, you cover me and I'm going in there and destroy them." So all I had was two thermite grenades –

Opposite: View looking eastward across the Pointe. Rudder's command post can be seen on the cliff side in the middle distance with visitors standing around. German counter-attacks came from the direction of the trees on the right, which in 1944 was open ground. *(DN)*

his and mine. I went in and put the thermite grenades in the traversing mechanism, and knocked out two of them because that melted their gears in a moment. And then I broke their sights, and we ran back to the road, which was a hundred or so yards back, and got all the thermites from the remainder of my guys manning the roadblock, and rushed back and put the grenades in the traversing mechanisms, elevation mechanisms, and banged the sights. There was no noise to that. There is no noise to a thermite, so no one saw us, and Jack said "Hurry up and get out of there Len," and I came up over the hedgerow with him and suddenly the whole place blew up.'

Source: Personal account on 'American Experience of D-Day' website: <www.pbs.org/wgbh/amex/dday/sfeature>.

The explosion was caused by a patrol from E Company, who had located and blown up the guns' ammunition. With these actions the Rangers had achieved their main aims.

Over the day the positions along the hedgerows came under attack, possibly from gunners of 2/1260th Army Coastal Artillery Battalion and headquarters staff of III/726th Grenadiers from the Château de Jucoville to the south. It is also known that at 1825 hours on 6 June, 352nd Infantry Division ordered elements of I/914th Grenadiers, based around Osmanville, to attack the Rangers.

The positions along the coastal road were in fact abandoned in confusion by the Americans during attacks on the night of 6 June. After retiring to the cliff, only 90 Rangers remained capable of bearing arms. During 8 June, Rudder's besieged force was relieved by 2nd and

A view from the Rangers' forward positions, looking due west. Sgts Lomell and Kuhn discovered and disabled the 155-mm guns in a field about 200 metres away. In 1944 the field behind the nearest tree line was an orchard. *(SCT)*

5th Rangers with elements of 116th Infantry, and tanks of 743rd Tank Battalion. Thirteen men received the Distinguished Service Cross for their actions.

Defenders of Rudder's command post on 7 June. Helped by naval gunfire support, Rudder's men held out throughout that day. (USNA)

ENDING THE TOUR: An interesting way to end the tour is to drive westwards along the D514 to the modest seaside town of Grandcamp-Maisy. On the outskirts of the town beside the main road is a National Guard Memorial. This is dedicated to Sgt Frank Peregory of K Company, 116th RCT, who was awarded the Medal of Honor for his actions in clearing positions outside Grandcamp on 8 June. Peregory was killed six days later, unaware of this award.

In Grandcamp-Maisy visit the *Musée des Rangers*. This has various exhibits relating to the Rangers, from their creation in Northern Ireland in June 1942 through to Pointe du Hoc.

Another site of interest is the German cemetery at la Cambe. With 21,160 burials, it is the largest German cemetery in France. The route is well signposted: take the D514 to Grandcamp-Maisy and the turn left on to the D199. Shortly after the bridge over the N13 dual carriageway, the road to the cemetery is on the left. Originally this was the site of US 29th Infantry Division's cemetery but the Americans were re-located to the site at Colleville-sur-Mer in 1947 (see pp. 184–5).

GRANDCAMP-MAISY RANGERS' MUSEUM

Musée des Rangers, 30 Quai Crampon, 14450 Grandcamp-Maisy; tel: +33 (0)2 31 92 33 51; web: www.normandy-dday.com>.
Open 1000–1900 Jun–Aug, 1000–1300 & 1500–1800 Apr–May & Sept (closed Mon low season). Admission charge.

VIERVILLE-SUR-MER: DOG-I EXIT

OBJECTIVE: This tour covers the assault against the western exit from Omaha Beach (Dog-1) in front of Vierville-sur-Mer by elements of the Provisional Ranger Force and 1st Battalion, 116th Regimental Combat Team, 29th Infantry Division.

DURATION/SUITABILITY: With a reasonably early start this tour will last into early afternoon, allowing time for lunch and a visit to the museum. Time taken will be reduced if a car is used to reach Stand B3, the furthest from Vierville. For those with mobility difficulties all stands are accessible by vehicle, but the alternative locations for Stands B1 and B2 are on the beach and will be difficult to reach. All stands can be reached by bicycle.

STARTING THE TOUR: The tour starts on the beach front at Vierville-sur-Mer. The most likely approach route is northwards from the main N13 road at Formigny, passing through the hamlet of les Isles and beside l'Ormel manor house on the D30 and entering Vierville from the south. About 300 metres past the church is the junction with the D514. Turn left (west) and after 100 metres you will see the entrance to the Avenue de Bedford (VA) on the right. This leads down to the Dog-1 draw. There is a large car park at the bottom of the draw and cars can also park closer to the seafront beside the National Guard Memorial. The Vierville draw and beach are the historical location for the opening scenes of Steven Spielberg's film *Saving Private Ryan*.

Legend (top left):

② Dog-3 exit

a Musée D-Day Omaha
b Rue de Cauvigny
c Rue de la Mer
d St-André church
e Avenue de Bedford
f Comité du Débarquement Signal Memorial

Base map: IGN 1412OT

STAND B1: A COMPANY, 116TH RCT

DIRECTIONS: Walk towards the National Guard Memorial at the bottom of the draw. The memorial is built on top of WN-72. To the right is a plaque to the men of 121st Engineer Combat Battalion (ECB), who opened the road into Vierville on 6 June. Opposite the *Hôtel du Casino* is a small memorial to 58th Armored Field Artillery Battalion.

Walk east past the National Guard Memorial to the end of the grassed area in front where two footpaths intersect. A seawall with a shingle bank against it ran along the promenade road in 1944 and was topped by barbed wire. If the tide is out there is the option of walking onto the beach where the Americans landed. This gives a dramatic insight into the problem confronting the assault troops.

THE SITE: On the eastern side of the draw, just below the white bungalow two-thirds of the way up the bluff, is the opening of an observation post that formed part of WN-71. Running for 200 metres along the bluff, the defences consisted of nine machine-gun positions, two mortars and a light cannon. At the base of the draw beneath the National Guard Memorial is a casemate of WN-72, housing an 88-mm anti-tank gun. (The gun is still inside.) Fifty metres further west along the coast is a casemate with embrasures on either side (one is now built over) for a 50-mm gun capable of firing in either direction. Both casemates enfiladed the beach. Shoulder walls concealed both guns' muzzle flashes from observation from seaward.

A series of trenches studded with machine-gun pits ran between the gun positions back to the top of the bluff behind

Landing craft of the first waves stream towards the beach in Dog Sector. *(USNA)*

the *Hôtel du Casino*. A 2-metre high anti-tank wall, in two echeloned sections, beside the 88-mm casemate blocked the road to vehicles. Mines covered the front of this obstacle.

The western side of the draw was protected by WN-73. The square embrasure of an emplacement for a French 75-mm 1897 field gun can still be discerned in the cliff facing east. Trenches and dugouts ran along the cliffs for about 300 metres, enclosing a ruined seafront house within the position, known to the Allies as the 'Fortified House'. To the west a spur of cliffs known as le Bec et la Baie du Mont can be seen. WN-74, located here, was armed with two 75-mm guns enfilading the beach and its approaches.

All in all, the defences at Vierville were probably the strongest on Omaha Beach.

THE ACTION: 1st Battalion, 116th Infantry's plan of attack was to assault with its four companies in column. A Company was to land first and clear the defences around the draw. B/116th would land 30 minutes later and assist A/116th, or move on to capture Vierville. C/ and D/116th would arrive at H+40 and H+50 respectively. The battalion would then advance west, link up with the Rangers at Pointe du Hoc, and eventually push on some 24 km to the outskirts of Isigny-sur-Mer. This plan never came close to success. By nightfall on 6 June 1/116th Infantry had penetrated no farther than the outskirts of Vierville.

The tanks of B Company, 743rd Tank Battalion, began landing on Dog Green and White beaches ahead

View of the Dog-1 exit looking west towards WN-72. The Type H667 casemate that housed the 88-mm PAK 43 is visible in the foreground, beneath the National Guard Memorial. In the background is one of the embrasures for the 50-mm gun. Behind, on top of the bluffs, is WN-73. *(TB)*

of the infantry at around 0629 hours. The rough seas had convinced Lt Dean Rockwell, USNR, commander of LCT Group 35, not to launch the DD tanks, but to land them from LCTs on the beach. The company commander was killed and four tanks lost when an LCT was sunk during the approach. As the remaining 12 Shermans landed and engaged German positions from the shallows, four were hit by fire from 88-mm and 75-mm guns at WN-72 and WN-74.

A/116th landed at 0636 hours on either side of WN-72. Many of the men were soaked and exhausted by seasickness. One of the six LCAs of 551st Landing Craft Assault Flotilla had already foundered but, despite each man carrying 60 lb of equipment, all but one of the 31-strong boat team were rescued.

A/116th's problems increased as the men arrived at the beach. The preliminary bombardment had been ineffective or missed its targets and a sandbar forced the men to disembark 30 metres from shore and wade the rest of the way. When the lead boat team, led by company commander Captain Taylor N. Fellers, were 250 metres from WN-72 the machine guns on the flanks opened fire to devastating effect. Fellers (who had discharged himself from hospital to lead his men) and his whole team from *LCA 910* died.

Over the next half an hour, until B/116th arrived in the second wave, A/116th was destroyed. Many men were cut down in the open. Groups of men sought cover behind tanks or damaged landing craft but German mortar operators proved adept at concentrating fire against

View from the National Guard Memorial on top of WN-72's 88-mm gun casemate. The extent of the tidal flat which the men of 116th RCT had to cross under fire suggests the size of the task they faced. Also evident is the excellent field of fire possessed by the 88-mm right along the curve of the beach. *(TB)*

these positions. Many wounded men on the beach were killed as German machine gunners continued to fire at any Americans they could see, ruthlessly searching for the living. Others who might have survived were drowned as the rising tide flowed over their incapacitated bodies.

In the chaos even the most determined soldiers could not fight back effectively. Sand jammed many rifles; only a few scattered rounds from one mortar were fired – the rest of the company's mortars were lost or lacked ammunition. And, even when fire was returned, lack of numbers, cohesion and visible targets rendered it ineffectual. Troops observed in action quickly drew return fire from the Germans. Many of those who reached the seawall were too wounded, physically and mentally, to organise an attack.

The arrival of the headquarters boat team 19 minutes later, and soon after elements of B/116th in the second wave, did not help. They suffered the same fate as A/116th.

Private Robert Sales, B Company, 116th Infantry, related his experience of the landing.

'The only words from the coxswain were: "I cannot go in any further. I'm going to drop the ramp." There was no argument about it. There were obstacles in the water. The water was up to my neck when I finally got my feet on the ground. He [the British coxswain] could not do any better... Then the ramp went down and these were the only words I heard the coxswain speak, and I do not know to this day whether he got

WN-72 from the jetty at the Vierville draw. The second firing embrasure of the 50-mm gun can be seen at the bottom right at the edge of the seawall where a white door has been added for its modern use as a storage shed. WN-71 was situated on the bluff top around the white bungalow, where an observation post can still be seen in the bluff to the left. *(TB)*

out alive or not, but when that ramp went down mortar shells were hitting on both sides of us. Machine guns were all over the top of us, just like you were in a bee's nest. The Captain was the first man to get off the boat and he was hit on the ramp and fell into the water. Sergeant Wright was next off, followed by the first aid man. I was fourth off the boat. The sea was rough, the ramp banged up and down, and I caught my heel and went over the side into the water. When I got up, Captain Zappacosta was up and calling to me, "I'm hit!" He went down and I did not see him come up. His body was washed up on the beach later.'

Source: Interview by Kevin Elsby, <www.warchronicle. com/ correcting_the_record/ambrose_coxswains.htm>.

The victims of German artillery or anti-tank fire litter Dog Beach. American soldiers commented on the accuracy and speed with which the Germans were able to concentrate fire along the beach with devastating effect. *(USNA)*

Sales was the only survivor from his boat team and his account refutes allegations in some sources that Captain Ettore Zappacosta had to threaten the coxswain with his pistol to take the landing craft inshore. Using a log and the bodies of A/116th men around him as cover, Sales took two hours to reach the seawall, where he spent the rest of the day in shock.

Many of the follow-up waves landed far to the east. Several boats of D/116th landed between WN-70 and WN-71 on the boundary of Dog Green and Dog White.

This placed distant support on the remnants of A/116th's eastern flank, which had been exposed since H-Hour when G/116th failed to land on Dog White. Even so, little could be done to remedy the situation directly in front of the Dog-1 exit.

The failure of most (or all) of the gap clearing teams allocated to Dog Green to arrive at their intended destinations meant that lanes were not blown through the beach obstacles for craft in the follow-up waves. The dual threat from the obstacles and intense fire on Dog Green meant that after 0800 hours it was impossible to land on this area. Many units began to divert to other sectors. 293rd Joint Assault Signal Company (JASCO) and 3565th Ordnance Company abandoned attempts to land here. Other units including 81st Chemical Weapons Battalion, 58th Armored Field Artillery Battalion, 397th and 467th AAA Battalions and 121st and 149th ECBs suffered considerable losses in men and vehicles. The frontal assault at Dog-1 was a complete failure.

Report of the commander of *Stützpunkt le Guay*, observing the situation on Omaha.

'At the water's edge at St Laurent and Vierville-sur-Mer the enemy is in search of cover behind the coastal obstacles. A great many vehicles – among them ten tanks – stand burning on the beach. The obstacle demolition squads have given up their activity. Debarkation from the landing boats has ceased, the boats keep farther to seawards. The fire of our strong points and artillery was well placed and has inflicted considerable casualties among the enemy. A great many wounded and dead lie on the beach.'

Source: 352nd Division telephone log, quoted in *Fighting the Invasion: The German Army at D-Day*, ed. David C. Isby, p. 195.

By the end of the day, 102 men of A/116th from a nominal strength of 193 were dead.

STAND B2: THE 'FORTIFIED HOUSE'

Above: The cliffs west of the Dog-1 exit on Charlie beach. This was the area where C/2nd Rangers, and HQ Company, 1/116th RCT, landed under heavy fire. WN-73 was situated directly on top of this stretch of cliff around the 'Fortified House', which lay in the gap visible in the cliff top. (SCT)

DIRECTIONS: Walk about 400 metres west along the beach. Look carefully for a substantial gap in the top portion of the cliffs. This was the location of a house, mistakenly termed the 'Fortified House' by the Allies. Then walk back along the path in front of the cliffs until you reach a path running inland up a small valley. Halfway up is the firing position for the French 75-mm gun. For small parties this can make a useful viewing point on to the beach. For those with mobility difficulties the base of the cliffs is accessible by car via the Rue de la Percée, running in front of the *Hôtel du Casino*.

THE ACTION: C Company, 2nd Rangers, was tasked to land on Dog Green three minutes behind A/116th. If A/116th captured Vierville quickly the Rangers were to pass through to assault the radar station on Pointe et Raz de le Percée. If A/116th failed, or was delayed, the Rangers were to scale the cliffs west of Dog Green and continue to their objectives.

Opposite: View of the ruins of the 'Fortified House'. The structure has been demolished since this photograph was taken, although access to the remaining emplacements of WN-73 can be made via the caravan and camping park to the rear. (SCT)

There is some confusion as to whether the Rangers made their rendezvous with the LCAs from HMS *Empire Javelin* carrying A/116th. The most reliable source, Sub-Lt George Green, commanding the craft from the *Empire Javelin*, states that the Rangers were late and he headed for shore without them. What is not disputed is that the landing experienced by C Company, 2nd Rangers, in *LCA 1038* and *LCA 418* was very similar to that of A/116th. Approaching to the west of the Dog-1 exit on Charlie Beach, a sandbar prevented the LCAs running on to the beach and forced the Rangers to disembark into chest-deep water. As the first men left *LCA 418*, a succession of mortar rounds struck the craft,

Left: A 1996 view of the 'Fortified House' (since demolished) from the base of the cliffs. It was slightly to the west of this location that 1st Lt Moody and two sergeants scaled the cliff using bayonets to secure a route off the beach. *(SCT)*

which quickly foundered. Only 30 out of 68 men reached the cover afforded by the base of the cliffs.

In the light of these losses, heavy fire obstructing movement towards Dog-1, and his inability to contact A/116th by radio, C Company's commander, Captain Ralph E. Goranson, ordered his remaining men up the cliffs. 1st Lt William B. Moody and two sergeants found a crevice in a slope to the west of the 'fortified house'. Under

fire they climbed up, pulling each other up and using their bayonets as hand-grips in the cliff face. After the leaders fixed toggle ropes near the top the rest of the Rangers ascended and then attacked German positions around the 'Fortified House' to relieve pressure on Dog Green.

Some 40 minutes after the Rangers' landing, 1/116th's HQ group arrived in four boats. Casualties were particularly heavy because the craft landed in succession, allowing the Germans to concentrate fire on each boat in turn. Only about 30 per cent of the men survived.

According to one account, at about 0830 hours Major Tom Dallas, battalion executive officer, ordered Lt Wayward C. Hooks to collect the remaining fit men and join B Company's men to scale the cliff. Other accounts state that B Company advanced under orders from Captain Goranson atop the cliff. Whatever may be the case, for the rest of the day these troops fought a series of actions amongst WN-73's trench complex. The position was finally secured around 1700 hours at a cost of only two further casualties; 69 Germans were killed. These troops were most likely from 11/726th Grenadiers, stationed at Vierville. Men from construction units were probably encountered after 1110 hours when III/726th reported that it had sent them to reinforce WN-71 and WN-73, since these were weakened by losses.

For much of the day the wounded lay amongst the rocks on the beach under sustained fire until WN-73 was neutralised. The intensity of the fire was such that, although Major Dallas lay only 100 metres from 1/116th's commander, Lt Col John A. Metcalfe, they could only communicate by radio. Loss of most of the radios, especially those of the Naval Shore Fire Control Party, prevented troops requesting fire from the destroyers off shore.

Around 0800 hours, seeing that the troops were pinned down along the beach, destroyer commanders closed the shore to fire at targets of opportunity. Off Charlie Beach, USS *McCook* neutralised the guns firing from WN-74; one emplacement was observed falling into the sea at about 0948 hours. USS *Carmick* fired by observing the fall of shot from tanks on Dog White firing at Dog-1. Unfortunately, one of the destroyers mistakenly fired on the men along the foot of the cliffs. About 1700 hours the bombardment ended when a beachmaster located a working radio. Dallas estimated that he lost more men at the base of the cliffs to the US Navy's fire than to the Germans'.

STAND B3:
THE ADVANCE TO VIERVILLE-SUR-MER

DIRECTIONS: Return to the main road near the National Guard Memorial. Join the Rue de Cauvigny, which runs along the beach east towards the village of les Moulins. Continue along for approximately 1,800 metres, until about 500 metres from the sail-shaped D-Day Memorial clearly visible on the seafront at les Moulins. On your right keep a close look out for a memorial to the site of the first US cemetery on Omaha Beach. This is set back from the road in front of a low light grey house. Stand in front of the memorial and look back west along the bluffs and beach towards Vierville. This is the area where elements of 116th RCT and 5th Rangers landed and advanced off the beach to take Vierville from flank and rear.

THE ACTION: Tides, poor visibility and navigation problems brought C/116th Infantry ashore some 10 minutes early,

Combat engineers kneel in prayer at a Sunday Mass on Dog Beach, 25 June 1944. The first American cemetery to be constructed in France is in the centre background. *(USNA)*

Memorial by the Rue de Cauvigny between Vierville and les Moulins. It was in this area that Brig Gen Cota inspired C/116th RCT to blast through the barbed wire and ascend the bluffs. (DN)

THIS MARKS THE SITE OF FIRST AMERICAN CEMETERY IN FRANCE WORLD WAR II SINCE MOVED TO AMERICAN CEMETERY N: I

Emplacement du I* cimetière américan Débarquement de Juin 1944

1** Infantry Division
29* Infantry Division
5* Engineer Special Brigade
6* Engineer Special Brigade

around 0710 hours, approximately 1,100–1,400 metres east of Vierville on Dog White. One of the six landing craft was tipped on its side by rough seas, and another took 20 minutes to free itself from a mined obstacle, but C/116th suffered only five or six casualties crossing the beach. However, as the men lay behind the cover of the seawall they were confused by the absence of key landmarks. Under fire they gradually became immobilised.

Initially the only other units on Dog White were five DD tanks, of which three were quickly knocked out. Over the next hour elements of 149th and 147th ECBs and 293rd Signal Company landed. The latter two units lost most of their equipment coming ashore, and 45 men were killed or wounded when their LCT was hit by artillery. C Company and two platoons of A Company, 147th ECB, moved west along the beach towards their intended landing site on Dog Green. The former dug in near the draw, whilst the A Company men joined infantry moving up the bluffs near Dog-1.

LCI 91, disembarking men of 116th RCT, was struck twice by shells that blew off the bow and set the craft ablaze when a flamethrower operator received a direct hit. Minutes later *LCI 92*, having failed to land on Easy Red, was set on fire by two mines as it tried to ram through the submerged beach obstacles. Many of the passengers, from 147th ECB, 149th Battalion Beach Group of the 6th Engineer Special Brigade, and two platoons from 214th Military Police Company, suffered burns and shock.

The final major unit to land was 5th Rangers under Lt Col Max Schneider. Having received no signal to land at Pointe du Hoc the Rangers had made their way to Dog Green. Seeing the destruction at that sector, Schneider brought his men in on the relatively quiet Dog White area. Only five or six men out of 450 were lost crossing to the seawall. Between 0750 and 0800 hours, for the first time in 116th RCT's half of the beach, effective combat units had reached the shore.

Slightly to the west the 116th RCT's command team landed from *LCVP 71*. Initially they took shelter amongst tanks of C Company, 743rd Tank Battalion, busy engaging positions firing at them from the area of Vierville, rather than WN-74, whose guns were left unhindered to fire at landing craft. Observing the troops pinned behind the seawall and amongst the groynes (which are still visible today), 116th RCT's commander, Col Canham, and 29th Infantry Division's Assistant Commander, Brig Gen Cota, set off to exhort the men to move off the beach before artillery fire zeroed in on them. Lt Col Schneider may also have helped initiate the Rangers' advance. What is clear is that C/116th did receive direct orders from Cota to advance, and that around the same time (0810 hours) the Rangers also attacked.

Private Ingram E. Lambert of C/116th was killed setting a bangalore torpedo amongst the barbed wire along the promenade road. 2nd Lt Stanley M. Schwartz managed to detonate the weapon on the second attempt. Five or six gaps in all were swiftly blown using bangalores. Witnesses in C/116th report that Canham was wounded in the wrist whilst using wire-cutters to open a gap, though confusingly some after-action interviewees from the company claim not to have seen the colonel at this time. After receiving first aid Canham continued to lead his men, urging them on at all opportunities.

Cota's contribution was no less critical or inspiring. Witnessing C/116th's advance stall when the first man through the gap in the wire was killed, Cota himself ran through. Soon the rest of C/116th followed his example. Threading through a network of trenches under light fire,

View of the bluffs over which elements of 116th RCT and 5th Rangers attacked. The undulating nature of the terrain, combined with smoke from fires started accidentally by naval gunfire, screened the troops from German fire. *(TB)*

Debris litters Dog Beach soon after 6 June. The ordered boxes of demolition charges and row of 'jerry' cans indicate that salvage and beach clearance operations are under way, although the evidence of two bodies lying covered on stretchers near the centre of the photograph seems to indicate that the process is slow, possibly haphazard. The cover that the shingle bank offered to the assault troops can be seen to the left. *(IWM AP26916)*

groups of men crossed 100 metres of grassland to reach the base of the bluffs, which they began to ascend via several slight paths. Casualties were light because of the weak German presence, folds in the ground that gave cover, and fires on the bluffs that obscured the advance from defences at Dog-3 and Dog-1. However, there was some opposition on top of the bluffs as various groups began to advance towards Vierville.

STAND B4: WN-70

DIRECTIONS: Retrace your route along the Rue de Cauvigny for about 800–1,000 metres. Look for a sign on the edge of the beach wall denoting the boundary between Dog Green and Dog White. Walk slowly west about 100 metres more until you see a path, shaped like a V laid on its side, running down the bluff to the right of a large red tiled house with a partly 'mock-Tudor' front, set back from the road behind a wall topped by a white fence. The path can be identified from the photo on page 146. The area above the house is the location of WN-70.

THE ACTION: At 0740 hours, A and B Companies, 2nd Rangers, waded ashore under mortar and machine-gun fire on Dog Green near WN-70. Some 68 men managed to reach the shingle bank and seawall. Although the Rangers thought they were alone, along the promenade road towards Vierville were tanks of A Company, 743rd Tank Battalion, engaged in a costly duel with WN-72 and WN-74. Mixed in with them were elements of B/116th and D/116th, with 121st ECB, many of whose men had sought cover at the seawall, or in the water.

D Company, 116th Infantry, lost heavily on its approach. This time the Germans had zeroed their machine

Taken around midday on 6 June, this photo shows Dog Green and a fraction of Dog White sectors. The trenches of WN-70 are visible on the right (east) side, above the houses. Along the promenade to the left are tanks of 743rd Tank Battalion, probably of B and A Companies, which engaged positions at Vierville and WN-74 respectively. The house in the middle, which was gutted by the Germans in preparation for demolition some time before the invasion, is shown on p.146 as it is today. *(Keele University Air Photo Archive)*

To the left of the house of the Hardelay family, whose walls were still standing on 6 June, can be seen the path used by the Germans to reach the beach from WN-70, which was situated on top of the bluff behind the house. *(DN)*

guns on the LCVPs' ramps as they approached the beach. Only 8 or 10 men out of 31 from 2nd Platoon's second section reached the seawall. Two craft were lost close offshore; one swamped and the second hit a mine. Another boat team disembarked, but suffered heavy loss when their officer, seeing troops crouching in the surf ahead ordered his men to do the same. Over the following 90 minutes constant fire meant that only half the group reached the seawall.

On Captain Arnold's orders the Rangers crossed the road, seeking cover amongst destroyed villas at the base of the bluffs. One group from B Company attempted to approach the Dog-1 draw, but was driven back by fire. A Company and the rest of B moved up the bluffs, screaming and firing at German positions. This group of Rangers was probably assisted by a heavy weapons platoon from D/116th that had landed 900 metres east of Vierville. The attack was spearheaded by an advance force of five Rangers, three of whom were killed clearing positions on the crest. According to after-action interviews, the D/116th men and Rangers then attacked a system of trenches, machine-gun posts, dug-outs and shelters directly overlooking landing positions on the beach. They killed six Germans and took 15 prisoners. Progress further west along the bluff was prevented by barbed wire and a machine-gun position so the troops moved inland to join Col Canham, seen advancing south towards Vierville.

Circumstantial evidence makes it overwhelmingly likely that the position attacked was WN-70, the only significant network of defences on this part of the bluffs.

Other groups advancing along the bluffs noted that the position had been neutralised. Captain Robert Walker, 1st Division liaison officer to 29th Division, described finding Germans killed by small arms and grenades roughly in the WN-70 area. However, as none of the accounts make reference to emplacements for heavy guns, it cannot be stated for certain that WN-70 was captured in this action.

STAND B5:
VIERVILLE-SUR-MER: OPENING DOG-1

DIRECTIONS: Travel back along the Rue du Cauvigny and up the Avenue de Bedford (VA) towards Vierville and the junction with the D514. On the way up the draw one of WN-71's machine-gun positions set into the top of the bluff to cover the exit road is visible on the left. On the wall along the right hand side is a plaque to 5th Rangers. It was in this area that Maj Gen Gerhardt established 29th Infantry Division's HQ on the evening of 6 June. At the front and rear of the car park are, respectively, memorials to 29th Infantry Division and 6th Engineer Special Brigade. At the D514 junction turn east and go 100 metres to the junction with the D30 to Formigny. To the south is St-André church. North is the 1944 beach exit road, the Rue de la Mer.

View of Vierville looking west along the D514 to the western end of the village. The D30 road to Formigny is on the left. The area in the distance was the site of sharp fighting between B/116th RCT and German reinforcements. It was in this area that twins Roy and Ray Stevens, both of A/116th, agreed to meet after clearing the beach. Ray was killed on 6 June, but 50 years later his brother returned to the promised rendezvous. *(DN)*

THE ACTION: During the advance over the bluffs, 5th Rangers and C Company, 116th Infantry, were joined by elements of D/116th, G/116th, and H/116th. D/116th had landed on Dog White while the latter two, having landed on Easy Red, had moved along the beach under fire to Dog White. These units joined Canham's and Cota's advance. The close countryside and machine-gun and sniper fire made this a slow process. On several occasions Cota, after unsuccessfully urging officers and NCOs to get their men moving, was forced to lead from the front, spurring the troops into action. The confusion caused by the beach landings and movement over the bluffs split the advance into numerous small groups. Despite this, some time after 1000 hours, the first attackers entered the eastern side of Vierville.

There was little initial resistance. Near the top of the draw several hundred German backpacks and sets of equipment were discovered, confirming reports from the dozen or so locals who emerged from their shelters that German troops had fled during the pre-landing bombardment. Unaware of the fate of A Company in front of Dog-1, C Company advanced west through Vierville. As the leaders reached 400 metres west of the crossroads (near the *Musée D-Day Omaha,* see p. 149) they were pinned down by German fire. Unable to make progress against German positions camouflaged amongst the hedgerows, C Company formed a defensive position. There was a similar situation on the southern edge of the village. A platoon of B Company silenced German positions in fields to the east of l'Ormel farm. Later a counter-attack by several truckloads of German infantry, probably combat engineers, drove the men of B Company back to l'Ormel but,

Col Charles Canham is awarded the British Distinguished Service Order by Gen Montgomery. His calmness under fire convinced his men he was the best regimental commander in the US Army. (IWM B6546)

once reinforced by a platoon of Rangers, they could not be dislodged.

Later in the day the B Company group tried to reach their objective to the west but German fire stalled their move. The Ranger platoon, however, succeeded in reaching their comrades besieged at the Pointe du Hoc, giving false hope that the rest of 5th Rangers would arrive. In fact, 5th Rangers had to abandon an attempt at passing south of Vierville towards the Pointe. In the evening the Rangers joined units of 116th RCT and 149th ECB in defensive positions west of the church.

Around 1200 hours Brig Gen Cota, escorted by several of his staff, walked down the Dog-1 draw towards the beach. This coincided with the battleship USS *Texas* firing six 14-inch shells at Dog-1, causing a number of Germans to surrender to Cota's party. Over the next few hours at least another 54 surrendered. When Cota reached the seafront he was confronted by the carnage of the morning's fight. Lt Jack Shea (Cota's aide) estimated that in every 100 metres there were 35–40 dead bodies. Dodging fire from snipers, who would not be dislodged until 7–8 June, Cota came across men of 121st ECB about 200 metres from the draw near tanks of A/743rd Tank Battalion. Assured that the draw was now secured the engineers scavenged amongst the surf and along the shore for equipment to begin blasting through the anti-tank wall. At 1400 hours the Dog-1 exit was opened, although German artillery fire and troops infiltrating back into positions on the bluffs continued to inflict casualties on units moving through it.

ENDING THE TOUR: Vierville has a number of historic buildings worth seeing, most of which featured in the fighting. Situated by the road to Formigny is the

D-DAY MUSEUM

Musée D-Day Omaha, Route Grandcamp, 14710 Vierville-sur-Mer; tel: +33 (0)2 31 21 71 80; web: <www.battlefieldsww2.50megs.com/musee_d_day_omaha.htm>. Open 0930–1930 1 Apr–11 Nov, groups by arrangement all year. Entrance fee.

Following a failed attempt at 0800 hours on 6 June, self-propelled guns of 58th Armored Field Artillery Battalion finally landed on Dog Red at 1600 hours. Note the smoke from grass fires obscuring the bluffs in several sectors. The smoke on the extreme right is from the wreckage of *LCI 91* and *LCI 92*, hit at about 0800 hours and still burning some eight hours later. *(IWM PL25623)*

13th-century St-André church. This was badly damaged when USS *Harding* destroyed the steeple on an erroneous report that German snipers were there. Continuing south, about 500 metres on the left is the 16th-century fortified farmhouse, l'Ormel. This was the location of fighting involving B/116th and 5th Rangers. American military maps mistakenly identified the buildings as the Château de Vaumicel. The actual château can be reached by walking 100 metres past l'Ormel onto the Chemin de Louvieries at the junction with the D30 and then right down the Rue de Vaumicel.

An alternative route is to walk west along the D514. On the left, opposite the Avenue de Bedford (VA) is the Manoir de Than. Before D-Day this was the commandant of Vierville's residence and was also used by 11/726th Grenadiers. A plaque notes that it then became the HQ of 11th Port. Some 400 metres west along the D514 is the *Musée D-Day Omaha*.

DOG RED TO EASY RED AND ST-LAURENT-SUR-MER

OBJECTIVE: This tour covers the landings around the Dog-3 and Easy-1 exits that led to the key village of St-Laurent-sur-Mer. The area was assaulted by elements of 1st and 29th Infantry Divisions. 1st Infantry Division's Assistant Commander, Brig Gen Wyman, described the capture and opening of the Easy-1 exit as the key to the battle for Omaha.

DURATION/SUITABILITY: The duration of the tour depends on the method of transport used. By vehicle a morning should be sufficient. On foot, or by bicycle (which can access all stands) it will more likely last into mid-afternoon, including a break for lunch and a museum visit. Those with mobility difficulties may have problems reaching Stand C2 as this involves climbing the bluffs via steep steps and an earth track. An alternative position is suggested.

STARTING THE TOUR: The tour starts on the beach front at les Moulins. The most likely approach route is to exit the N13 at Formigny. Go north into Formigny village and at the crossroads just past the church take the right fork towards St-Laurent-sur-Mer, the D517. Stay on this road through St-Laurent following the signs to 'Normandie 1944: D-Day; Le Choc'. On arriving at les Moulins, there are are two large car parks to the left and right of the roundabout at the bottom of the draw.

STAND C1:
ASSAULT ON THE DOG-3 EXIT

DIRECTIONS: Walk from the car park to the large stone monument at the seafront that commemorates the Allied landings on Omaha. This marks the border between beach sectors Dog Red (west) and Easy Green (east). On the sides of the monument are plaques to 1st and 29th Infantry Divisions. At the seafront just west of the monument is a plaque commemorating Operation 'Aquatint'. This was an unsuccessful British commando raid in August 1942 intended to capture prisoners for intelligence purposes. From the monument face inland to look at the bluffs on either side of the Dog-3 exit.

If the tide is out, move out onto the beach to gain a better sense of the task facing the American forces. WN-66 and WN-68 were on the eastern and western sides of Dog-3 exit respectively. Both positions had emplacements atop and at the base of the bluffs. In front of them across the draw ran an anti-tank ditch, while an anti-tank wall blocked the valley farther inland.

THE ACTION: The Dog-3 draw in front of les Moulins was to be opened by 2nd Battalion, 116th Infantry. The battalion would then move to higher ground to the south of Vierville, whilst the follow-up waves of 3/116th and 115th RCT exploited south to positions overlooking the flooded River Aure valley. The failure to open Dog-3 until late on 6 June frustrated these plans, forcing the Americans to shift their thrust to the east through the Easy-1 and Easy-3 draws and dislocating the advance inland.

Landings at H-Hour on Dog Red and Easy Green initially went relatively smoothly compared to most other sectors on Omaha. A Company, 743rd Tank Battalion, landed and deployed to provide covering fire for the Special Engineer Task Force's gap demolition teams, tasked to blow paths through beach obstacles for follow-up waves of landing craft. Many of the engineers landed further to the east, but a number of teams did begin operations in front of les Moulins. Team 4 suffered heavy casualties and Team 5 was unable to blow its charges because of infantry sheltering amongst the obstacles. By 0640 hours, the first gap had been cleared at Dog-3 by Team 6, but losses from German fire and the rising tide soon forced the gap demolition teams to stop work and take cover by the seawall. Throughout the day 743rd Tank Battalion's tanks engaged German defences. Three Shermans overran WN-68's forward positions; later in the day some A Company tanks advanced to the Vierville draw, which they passed through that evening.

The assault infantry companies, arriving between 0635 and 0639 hours, met mixed success. E/116th landed to the east in 16th RCT's sector. F/116th and G/116th's craft were scattered on either side of the junction of Dog Red and Easy Green. Four sections from G/116th and three from F/116th landed on Dog Red. G/116th's sections crossed the beach in as little as four minutes, suffering light casualties from ill-directed and sporadic German fire – smoke from fires on the bluffs obscured them from WN-68. F/116th, landing slightly to the east, was not covered by smoke; consequently it suffered heavier casualties, though the advance still crossed the beach quickly.

These two groups soon began a series of moves that carried them over the bluffs and west towards Vierville, during which they linked up with elements of 5th Rangers and 1/116th, who had penetrated inland from Dog White (*see Stand B3*). In most cases these advances became erratic and disorganised. G/116th's problems began when it was ordered to move 1 km westward to its target, Dog White. As the sections moved along the beach under artillery and mortar fire, through areas crowded with men wounded and in shock, cohesion collapsed.

Along the rest of beach in front of les Moulins attacks failed to progress as successfully. At 0700–0705 hours Headquarters Company, 2/116th, had landed on Dog Red. H/116th arrived at the same time, but found its sections scattered as far east as Easy Red. After-action interviews with Captain Charles R. Cawthorn, HQ Company commander, and Chaplain Captain Charles D. Reed, related that, as these units approached the beach, the men's confidence grew as there were few sounds of battle and nothing appeared untoward. Any such views quickly evaporated.

Major Sidney V. Bingham, Jnr., commander 2/116th Infantry, recalled his landing on Dog Red at les Moulins.

'I thought all was well until after struggling ashore through shoulder-deep water, I paused for a breather behind a steel tetrahedron anti-boat obstacle and noticed the sand kicking up at my feet... I was getting shot at... From then on, there was no doubt in my mind. I was scared, exhausted... I finally crossed the beach and got to the shingle along the beach road where about 100 men from F Company were seeking what little shelter the road afforded.'

Source: Cited in Tim Kilvert-Jones, *Omaha Beach: V Corps's Battle for the Normandy Beachhead*, p. 124.

C Company, 149th ECB, landing at 0705–0720 hours, found it difficult to carry out its tasks of cutting wire and making a road through the dunes. One officer led a detachment to the foot of the bluffs but German fire prevented them climbing up. With the beach exit closed and obstacles still in place, follow-up waves found it difficult to land. Those that did reach the shore came under heavy anti-tank and artillery fire. Men from 95th Quartermaster Battalion landing on Easy Green were confronted by burning fuel and ammunition trucks. 111th Field Artillery Battalion could not land its guns from DUKWs on Dog Red/Easy Green at H+110

A view of WN-68, showing a machine-gun position that covered the western side of the Dog-3 exit. (TB)

Easy Red

Easy Green

St-Laurent-sur-Mer

la Fraisnaie

les Moulins

les Costils

FLOODED AREA

WN-65

WN-66

WN-68

WN-64

WN-67

WN-69

Cimetière
militaire
américain

Musée

les Fosses Taillis

To FORMIGNY & N13

D514

D517

D514

② Anti-tank wall
③ Dog-3 exit
④ Easy-1 exit
⑤ Elements 2 and 3/116th RCT
⑥ 2/115th RCT and 743rd Tank Battalion
⑦ 1/115th RCT
⑧ 3/115th RCT

a   Musée Omaha 6 Juin 1944
    Base map: IGN 1412OT

Kilometres
0   0.5   1

because of German resistance. The advance party which did land at 0700–0730 hours suffered heavy casualties. Lt Col Thornton L. Mullins and his men abandoned their tasks and set out trying to organise groups of infantry frozen behind the seawall. Mullins successfully directed a tank against a strongpoint. Soon afterwards he was shot in the stomach by a sniper, and took 12 hours to die. The 13 DUKWs carrying the battalion's guns were all lost during the morning. One gun, rescued before its DUKW sank, was all that landed from 11th Field Artillery (and was subsequently placed under command of 7th Field Artillery, which got six of its guns ashore).

Major Sidney Bingham constantly moved under fire amongst his men sheltering along the seawall trying to rouse and organise them. Bingham managed to lead forward a party from his headquarters and a section of F/116th lying idle after their officer had been wounded. They crossed Dog Red towards a three-storey house near WN-66 on Easy Green. Along the way Bingham met men from the first three sections of F/116th that had landed on the eastern side of Dog-3. Unprotected by smoke these units suffered 40 casualties during the 45 minutes it took to cross the beach. A number of the wounded drowned when the tide came in because they prematurely removed their life preservers on reaching the seawall, thinking it safe.

With just 50 men Bingham moved through the wire and the network of trenches in front of the house. The lack of any opposition here is puzzling. A likely explanation is that,

The view from the eastern extreme of Dog Red looking south-east towards the bluffs, where WN-66 was situated. The position ran down the bluffs to the level ground below, but two of the casemates here were still incomplete on 6 June. It was across this area that Major Bingham led elements of F/116th RCT. (TB)

with construction work unfinished and limited numbers of troops available, the Germans chose to concentrate on the finished sections of WN-66 on the bluff. Despite this, around 0800 hours an attempt to set up a fire-base against German positions on the bluff was thwarted by the fact that the men's weapons were all jammed. It proved impossible to contact the Navy Shore Fire Control Party and bombard the German positions, which were quick to concentrate their fire against any radio aerial that was set up. Bingham and ten men moved east of the house and infiltrated up the bluff but, unable to deal with a machine-gun nest with jammed weapons, they were forced to withdraw.

Later in the morning Bingham ordered the few officers around him still active to gather all available men and follow him east towards Easy-1. They managed to raise only 50 men, shock and exhaustion having enveloped most of the unwounded troops. Joined by elements of G/116th and M/116th they moved over the bluff to join 3/116th, which had already made a successful and rapid advance towards St-Laurent. For his actions on 6 June Bingham was awarded the Distinguished Service Cross.

The Dog-3 draw itself was finally secured in the evening when fire from destroyers completed the neutralisation of the German positions. Around 2030 hours Captain McGrath, of 116th RCT's Service Company, walked down the road from St-Laurent into les Moulins and met several

Knocked out US equipment litters Dog Beach, west of les Moulins, after the assault. The tank, named 'Ceaseless' by its crew, is from 743rd Tank Battalion's C Company. *(IWM PL26210)*

of his unit's vehicles driving up. With the Germans not yet cleared from the village and the head of the draw, he sent them east towards 1st Infantry Division's area.

STAND C2:
3/116TH RCT'S BREAKTHROUGH

DIRECTIONS: Follow the D517 east from les Moulins along the coast. After approximately 1 km the road gently curves slightly inland behind a number of beach houses. Continue to the car park at the entrance to the the Easy-1 draw where the D517 turns inland. At the base of the western side of the bluff is a casemate for a 50-mm gun belonging to WN-65. In front is a striking memorial to 2nd Infantry Division, commemorating its landing on 7 June. Behind the casemate a combination of steps and a path lead to the top of the bluff. Once at the top walk along the path west along the bluff's edge for about 400 metres, stopping where you can look over the beach and back across the fields to St-Laurent. When visited by the author, the area was rather overgrown so sturdy footwear is recommended. The path is shown on the IGN map as being part of the GR223 walking route, so there should be no problems with rights of access.

The stand will probably not be accessible to those with mobility difficulties. However, the grassed area near the car park abutting the dunes looks back down the line of the bluffs along the D517, giving at least some understanding of the area under attack. This position can also be used for Stand C3.

THE ACTION: 3/116th's four companies landed to the east of their intended beach sectors. I/116th and K/116th landed in relatively compact order on Easy Green. L/116th was dispersed between the Dog-3 and Easy-1 draws. M/116th landed across the front of the Easy-1 draw on Easy Red in 1st Infantry Division's zone. The landings took place between 0710 and 0727 hours with I/116th earliest and M/116th, as scheduled, last.

I/116th, K/116th and L/116th had similar experiences during the landing. Fire during the approach and on the beach was light. Men in I/116th claimed that it was five or six minutes before they noticed machine-gun fire around them. No craft were lost and casualties were modest; K/116th claimed no losses before reaching the seawall, though all the troops had to disembark into knee- or waist-high water because their landing craft were stopped by sandbars, or obstacles which engineers were still trying to clear. The worst landing was by 3rd Platoon, K/116th, whose men dumped their kit and swam ashore after the first man had plunged off the ramp and briefly vanished below the water.

Some men moved across the beach in bounds, but in general most ran in one attempt. I/116th's No. 4 boat team ducked under the water, working their way forwards, whilst Sgt Weston E. Carlson and Private William Boyd provided covering fire from the surf with a light machine gun. Boat teams from all three companies were quickly established along the seawall, perhaps in as little as five minutes. As one group of L/116th moved to a shell crater Private Shroudy had a fortunate escape, being wounded when a bullet that struck the area of his heart was deflected by a coin. Many in L/116th felt that Private Pearl M. Robertson deserved to be posthumously decorated for his calm courage as he tried to engage a suspected machine-gun position.

K/116th found the seawall empty, but men of I/116th and L/116th discovered themselves among men of G/116th who

A view from WN-68 of the Dog-3 exit. In the distance can be seen the ground which I, K and L/116th RCT eventually managed to cross to scale the bluffs. *(DN)*

The view from the German trenches on top of the bluffs between the Easy-1 and Dog-3 draws. The photo was probably taken from WN-65, looking onto Easy Red, although one source claims it was taken at WN-66. *(IWM PL26536)*

were immobilised, although one sergeant noted that they seemed in good condition.

Reports of the companies' assault on the bluffs differ as to the timing, and describe a lack of co-ordination between the sections. K/116th reported that it delayed at the seawall until 0830–0900 hours, and that it reached the top of the bluffs around 1230 hours; L/116th claimed to have reached the top around 1030 hours; I/116th reports do not note the time of the assault, only that it took 30 minutes for the lead section to complete. In most cases it was junior officers who began the advance on their own initiative. Deciding there were already too many men along the seawall, L/116th's Lt Donald C. Anderson was one who urged his men forward; he was later shot through the head by a sniper.

Orders that 3/116th's companies were not to form up from their boat sections, but press rapidly inland to the battalion assembly area, possibly assisted them in carrying out their attack. Accepting that they would move in small isolated sections, the three companies were ideally suited in terms of deployment and mentality to carry out an improvised assault.

I/116th's advance was broadly typical of the other units. Two of the company's boat sections were equipped for beach assault. 3rd Section was able to cut through some thin wire but, faced with a thicker obstacle, 4th Section found it necessary to blast a hole with four bangalores. I/116th's other sections then followed through the gaps, scaling steep bluffs in what became a single column in order to avoid mines. Casualties varied, but none of the companies suffered severely. K/116th's passage from the seawall to the base of the bluffs was covered by sand dunes, but then delayed by a marsh. There were numerous mines, but it seems that here the rockets fired from the LCT(R)s had blown the wire successfully and destroyed or exposed many mines.

Along the top of the bluff the various groups moved forwards independently, generally towards St-Laurent. Most came under machine-gun and small arms fire from a hedgerow some 300 metres inland. After knocking out two machine-gun positions with demolition charges L/116th probed slowly forwards to the road junction at the entrance of the les Moulins valley, 300 metres north of the modern D517/D514 junction.

K/116th's advance was made in two groups. The largest group of 100 men joined L/116th, but two sections managed to reach 116th RCT's regimental headquarters at Vierville. Forty men of I/116th managed to fight their way through to the battalion assembly area. During this advance Private Boyd used his BAR to kill 15–20 Germans whose fire was hindering the advance north of St-Laurent, enabling the rest of the unit to clear the position, taking eight prisoners. By evening this group had been joined by the majority of 3/116th and elements of 2/116th, including Major Bingham. Resistance from elements of 5th and 8th Companies, 916th Grenadiers and 10th Company, 726th Grenadiers, finally halted their advance near WN-67 and WN-69.

STAND C3: ENGINEERS AT EASY-1 EXIT

DIRECTIONS: Walk back east along the path to where it descends to the Easy-1 exit. For Stand C3 you can either remain at the top of the bluff or descend to the casemate below. From either location observe the line of dunes beyond the houses between the D517 road and the beach. Also note the bluff on the eastern side of Easy-1 draw;

this was the site of WN-64, although trees cover the position. Beyond is the American Cemetery.

THE ACTION: From 0625–0635 hours, gap assault teams began landing on Easy Red in the vicinity of the Easy-1 draw. During the next 30 minutes they struggled to open gaps for follow-up landing waves, suffering heavy casualties in the process. Team 11 had seven men killed when its rubber boat packed with explosives erupted in a fireball, detonated by shrapnel. American infantry sheltering behind beach obstacles stopped Team 12 from blowing its gap; despite three cries of 'fire in the hole' the troops would not move. Most of the team and many of the troops were killed or wounded when a German round set off the charges. Team 13 took casualties in a similar way. By 0700 hours, when the tide forced the gap assault teams off the beach, only one marked passage was available.

After 0700 hours, elements of 37th and 149th ECBs arrived to open routes inland from the beach. 348th ECB

Above: A view of Fox Green sector and the eastern sector of Easy Red, with WN-62 under fire on the right-hand side and WN-61 burning fiercely in the centre. Anti-tank guns at the former position inflicted heavy losses on tanks supporting 116th RCT's attack against the Easy-1 draw. *(USNA)*

Right: Air photos of Easy Red, taken (*top*) around midday, and (*below*) about 1500 hours on 6 June. In the upper photo there are numerous vehicles and infantrymen on the beach. Other vehicles can be seen landing and forming into organised groups while landing craft plough as close to the shore as they dare through the submerged German obstacles. In the lower photo the tide has gone out and some German obstacles can still be seen in places on the beach. These would continue to be cleared during the following 24 hours by C/149th ECB and B/37th ECB. Two bulldozers can be seen working inland through the shingle bank and dunes towards the beach track running parallel to the shore. *(Keele University Air Photo Archive)*

units also landed on Easy Red instead of Fox Green. German fire hindered their ability to work. The beach between Dog-3 and Easy-1 became clogged with vehicles, many knocked out, as this was the only area with passages through the obstacles. To avoid further loss, between 0830 and 0900 hours (sources vary) the commander of the 7th Beach Battalion ordered landings to cease.

At 1400 hours landing of vehicles was resumed, and the critical axis of advance inland for Omaha was open. This was achieved through the neutralisation of WN-64 and WN-65, allowing the engineers to resume their tasks.

Men of M/116th were the first infantry to land in the vicinity of the Easy-1 draw around 0727 hours.

Though losses crossing to the shingle bank were light, many accounts state that, on reaching a gully at the base of the bluff, M/116th remained there for much of the day. However, the unit's after-action report says that, after using automatic weapons and mortar fire to neutralise part of WN-65, it gradually infiltrated up the bluffs towards St-Laurent, rather than over-running WN-65.

The death blows to WN-65 came in three forms. Signallers of 293rd JASCO, unable to carry out their tasks, gave their radios to the infantry and began to fire on the casemate at the base of the bluffs with rifle grenades. Around 1030 hours, Sgt Hass, commanding a half-track of 467th AAA Automatic Weapons Battalion, though unable to cross the shingle managed to fire ten rounds at the casemate, shortly after which 20 Germans surrendered. Around 1130 hours infantry completed the reduction of the final position under cover of naval gunfire co-ordinated by one of the few functioning shore fire control parties. At 1140 hours, 726th Grenadier Regiment informed 352nd Infantry Division that Easy-1 draw had been breached.

In front of WN-65 is a memorial to 2nd US 'Indian Head' Infantry Division, which landed on D+1. *(TB)*

With WN-64 neutralised around the same time, the engineers were able to resume work. On the beach the gap assault teams of 146th and 299th ECBs were busy by mid-afternoon. By the end of 6 June five marked gaps were open between Easy-1 and Easy-3, opening Easy-1 to traffic. C/149th ECB, and B/37th ECB, bulldozed access roads through the shingle to the lateral beach road on either side of the draw. They also filled in the anti-tank ditch and began clearing mines in the draw, and the fields above the bluffs to the west, despite sniper fire. The grass track running up the western side of the draw (the present-day road) was also cleared and open to vehicles by late afternoon. However, the continued fighting in St-Laurent caused traffic jams and prevented a steady flow of vehicles inland.

Troops also began to flow through the draw. After 1100 hours 18th and 115th RCTs began landing on Easy Green and Easy Red to advance inland. At 1500 hours the command party of the Provisional Engineer Special Brigade Group landed and established its HQ in the casemate by the bluff, replacing forward headquarters of 1st Infantry Division which moved into the fields above. During the days and weeks after 6 June men of 6th Engineer Special Brigade transformed Easy-1 exit into a route-way for vast numbers of men, and huge quantities of supplies.

Captain Ian F. Fraser, Provisional Engineer Special Brigade Group, described logistic operations in late June.

'… yesterday almost 15,000 tons of cargo, some 3000 vehicles, and over 10,000 men were landed across this beach… The seawall is still black with ships lying outside and inside the artificial breakwater and between them and the shore orderly processions of DUKWs and ferry craft are transporting supplies, vehicles and men. The DUKWs run into crane-equipped transfer areas, where cargo is quickly shifted into trucks which then move in steady stream up each of the five main exits from the beach. Down return roads roll other trucks on their way back from inland dumps, ready to take their places in the lines at the transfer points or beside the rhino ferries or dumb barges beached along the sand… The thousands of mined obstacles have disappeared, too, and the anti-tank ditches, the barbed wire, and the houses wrecked by the pre-H-Hour bombardment. A two-lane road now runs the length of the beach, and numerous signs point the way to command posts and dumps and transit areas. Huge permanent markers identify each beach, so that now there is no reason why craft destined for Easy White should come ashore at Dog Red or Fox Green, as they did on D-Day.'

Source: Operation Neptune Report, Provisional Engineer Special Brigade, US National Archives.

WN-65, with
a memorial
plaque to 467th
AAA Automatic
Weapons
Battalion (Self-
Propelled), part of
18th AAA Group.
The top of the
casemate displays
the effects of
a probable hit
by naval gunfire,
which combined
with the fire
of 467th AAA
Battalion and
signallers of
293rd JASCO
to neutralise the
position. *(TB)*

Opposite: The
D517 road
running down
to les Moulins
from St-Laurent.
It was in this
area that L/116th
RCT's attack
was frustrated by
enemy fire. *(DN)*

STAND C4: ST-LAURENT-SUR-MER

DIRECTIONS: Travel along the road cut by American engineers on 6 June that runs south up the side of the Easy-1 exit. The road turns west onto the plateau and after 300 metres reaches a junction on the outskirts of St-Laurent. Take the left-hand fork, continue to the D514, join it heading west and drive 500 metres to the junction where the D517 leads down to les Moulins. There is a car park on the left.

The road running east back to St-Laurent (signposted Colleville-sur-Mer), and the fields behind were the axis of advance for 2/115th. The main German positions covering the beach road running down to les Moulins were sited to the north-west of the junction behind the houses on the western side of the beach road. WN-69, consisting of machine-gun and mortar positions, lay 300 metres to the west of the stand along the road to Vierville.

Those who wish a better view of the area of the action of elements of 3/116th covered in the first paragraph below should walk down the D517 towards les Moulins and the next junction, but this is not essential.

THE ACTION: The pattern of the fighting around St-Laurent during the afternoon of 6 June is difficult to relate accurately. At the northern crossroads nearest to les Moulins, elements of 3/116th failed to clear German forces in a series of actions. The common problem that hindered units in this area was the close nature of the terrain, which

made it difficult to locate and engage concealed German positions. M/116th was forced to withdraw towards St-Laurent because its mortars could not suppress the Germans with random fire. Inability to deliver accurate fire onto positions on the high ground to the west led to L/116th's attack down either side of the road towards les Moulins being pinned down with heavy losses. A captain from 293rd JASCO, observing the accuracy of the German artillery fire, determined that they had an observer in St-Laurent church steeple; naval gunfire demolished it. L/116th then fell back to the high ground above the junction and dug in for the night.

Unfortunately the naval gunfire against St-Laurent inflicted minor casualties on the men of 2/115th Infantry, who were trying to clear the village. 115th RCT's plan of attack was for 1/115th to move around to the south of the village and isolate it whilst 2/115th and 3/115th attacked. The fighting was confused, and after-action accounts do not always make it possible to identify which parts of the

Above: Looking north along the D517 across its junction with the D514 heading to Vierville (*left*) and Colleville (*right*). The fields behind the signposts right of centre marked the axis of advance for 2/115th Infantry. The German positions covering the road to les Moulins were beyond the houses to the left. *(TB)*

OMAHA 6 JUNE MUSEUM

Musée Omaha 6 Juin, Rue de la Mer, Les Moulins,
14710 St-Laurent-sur-Mer; tel: +33 (0)2 31 21 97 44;
web: <www. musee-memorial-omaha.com>.Open daily 1000–1230 &
1430–1800 15 Feb–15 Mar; 0930–1830 16 Mar–15 May & 16 Sept–15 Nov;
0930–1900 16 May–15 Sept (to 1930 in July & Aug). Entrance fee.

village were secured, by whom and at what times. Indeed from their accounts the battalions seem to have been unaware of each other's presence.

The advance suffered from a lack of artillery support, especially when elements of 3/115th approached the road junction on the Vierville road towards evening. Lt Col Cooper unsuccessfully tried to arrange support from 110th and 111th Field Artillery Battalions. However, the 110th was not yet ashore, and only one of the 111th's guns had survived. Captain Thomas Cadwalader managed to bring up several M7 Priest self-propelled guns of 58th Armored Artillery Battalion. In the evening these used their 105-mm guns to blast some Germans from the thick-walled stone buildings they occupied on the edge of St-Laurent.

K/115th, supported by a tank of 743rd Tank Battalion ordered from 1st Infantry Division to the east by Brig Gen Cota, attempted to clear the village and the position around WN-67 and WN-69. Arriving at the crossroads,

This scene of activity was photographed at the Easy-1 draw several days after the initial landings and shows French civilians helping American troops to stack life belts. In the centre background can be seen the remains of WN-64, and to its right WN-65. *(Todd/USNA)*

the tank briefly fired its machine guns and two 75-mm shells towards the Germans, but fire from an anti-tank weapon to the south forced it to retire. K/115th also withdrew from the centre of St-Laurent under fire, though I/115th later infiltrated back in under cover of darkness.

On several occasions in the afternoon and evening of 6 June Brig Gen Cota urged Col Eugene Slappey, commander of 115th RCT, to press his attacks to secure the village, and in particular the crossroads that were vital for opening Dog-3 draw to traffic. During the night Slappey established a fire base to support a major attack against WN-67 and WN-69. On 7 June the assault met little opposition as the Germans had mostly withdrawn during the night, though clearance operations continued throughout the day. Cota constantly urged the men on. In one instance he personally led an attack on a barn, threw in grenades and broke open the door. He then turned to the lieutenant and demanded to know if he now understood how to take a building.

ENDING THE TOUR: Drive back down the D517 towards les Moulins. On the left-hand side is the *Musée Omaha 6 Juin*, which is clearly signposted.

If time permits it is also worth visiting the *D-Day Museum* on the seafront at Arromanches-les-Bains, some 20 km east on the D514. This has an excellent display dealing with Mulberry B harbour built by the British, and gives an idea of what the American Mulberry A at Omaha would have looked like. If the tide is out remains of Mulberry B can be seen on the beach. Arromanches is a popular seaside resort and has numerous restaurants and shops making it easy to relax there for several hours.

D-DAY LANDING MUSEUM

Musée du Débarquement, Place du 6 Juin, 14117 Arromanches; tel: +33 (0)2 31 22 34 31; web: <www.musee-arromanches.fr>. See website for opening hours. Entrance fee.

THE BIG RED ONE

OBJECTIVE: This tour covers the landings of the US 1st Infantry Division ('The Big Red One') around the Easy-3 and Fox-1 exits. The Fox-1 exit was the first to be secured by American forces on 6 June, while the fighting around the WN-62 position proved to be some of the bitterest.

DURATION/SUITABILITY: The tour covers a relatively small section of the beach and the bluffs. On foot or by bicycle (which can gain access to all but Stand D3, which requires you to walk from the American Cemetery car park) it should take a morning, or slightly less by car. Those with mobility difficulties should note that Stands D2 and D3 can be reached by well-maintained paths from nearby car parks. D1 is reached by a shingle track that may be harder to negotiate.

STARTING THE TOUR: The tour commences on the beachfront to the east of the 'Village de Vacances' north of Colleville-sur-Mer. Exit the N13 at Formigny and follow the D517 to St-Laurent-sur-Mer. On the outskirts of St-Laurent turn right on to the D514 following the signs to Colleville for 3 km. Just past the church in Colleville turn left towards the beach, bearing left at the junction 300 metres along. At the base of the Easy-3 draw go right; where the road forks there are several parking areas.

STAND D1: ASSAULT ON THE FOX-1 EXIT

DIRECTIONS: After parking return to the main access road and walk east to the junction with the road leading to the 'Village de Vacances'. Here take the left turn leading to the beach and follow the shingle path east, paralleling the beach. After 200 metres a large casemate is visible on private property on the right. This was part of WN-61. WN-60 lay to the east above the simple white buildings part way up the bluff, beyond those with the russet slate roofs. The Fox-1 draw ran directly through the white buildings. If you wish to gain access to WN-60, walk along the grassy area above the beach and then follow the wide path uphill towards the south-west corner of the German position. Access into WN-60 is possible from this location. It is possible to see remnants of the defences here, and there is a signboard (unfortunately, not wholly accurate) that provides further details of the fighting that took place in this area.

THE ACTION: 1st US Infantry Division's plan called for 3/16th RCT to land in two waves, each with two companies abreast. The battalion was to break through the coastal defences and subsequently advance inland, seizing Ste-Honorine-des-Pertes and the crucial high ground of Mont Cauvin on the eastern boundary of V Corps' sector. Around 0600 hours the first wave began moving towards Omaha, followed at carefully timed intervals by successive waves.

Journalist and writer Ernest Hemingway gives an eye-witness report of the landings on Fox Green Beach at 0710 hours.

'No one remembers the date of the battle of Shiloh. But the day we took Fox Green beach was the sixth of June, and the wind was blowing hard out of the northwest. As we moved in toward land in the grey early light, the 36-foot coffin-shaped steel boat took

An infanteer's view of WN-62. The Engineer Special Brigade Memorial is visible atop one of WN-62's 75-mm gun casemates. *(TB)*

A wounded soldier of an unknown unit prepares to receive first aid from a medical officer on Fox Red. Clearly visible in the background are other troops, physically and emotionally exhausted, taking shelter under the cliff. *(USNA)*

solid green sheets of water that fell on the helmeted heads of the troops packed shoulder to shoulder in the stiff, awkward, uncomfortable, lonely companionship of men going into battle. There were cases of TNT, with rubber-tube life preservers wrapped around them to float them in the surf, stacked forward in the steel well of the LCV(P), and there were piles of bazookas and boxes of bazooka rockets encased in waterproof coverings that reminded you of the transparent raincoats college girls wear...

As the boat rose to a sea, the green water turned white and came slamming over the men, the guns and the cases of explosives. Ahead you could see the coast of France. The grey booms and derrick-forested bulks of the attack transports were behind now, and, over all the sea, boats were crawling forward toward France.'

Source: 'Voyage to Victory', in *By-Line: Ernest Hemingway*, ed. William White, p. 349.

Between 0630 and 0800 hours elements of five infantry companies landed on Fox Green and Fox Red in chaotic circumstances. First ashore were several sections from E/116th RCT and four from F/16th RCT, which should have landed on Easy Green and Easy Red respectively. Suffering heavy casualties crossing the beach, and with their sections scattered over a wide area, the two companies reached the cover of the shingle bank in considerable disorder. Most of E/116th RCT quickly became immobilised; in after-action interviews, survivors attributed their later advance inland to the example set by units of the combat-experienced 16th RCT. At 0700 hours K/16th RCT arrived on Fox Green, followed over the next hour by M and I/16th RCT. These three companies struggled ashore under fire, through water ranging from waist to neck high. Apart from one craft which swamped, L/16th RCT managed to get ashore under the cliffs along Fox Red with comparatively modest casualties, although the advance across the beach was as chaotic as in other sectors.

Despite the heavy casualties, by 0800 hours several assaults were underway to overcome the German positions at WN-60 and WN-61. At around 0800 hours, L/16th spearheaded an attack against WN-60 on top of the bluffs. Under the direction of Lt Robert R. Cutler, the 2nd, 3rd and 5th Sections began to advance up the Fox-1 draw lying to the west of WN-60. The attack was assisted by fire from destroyers and two Sherman tanks directed by 1st Lt Jimmie W. Monteith. For this action, and his role during fighting above the bluffs later, Monteith was posthumously awarded the Medal of Honor.

On reaching the top, 3rd and 5th Sections fanned out to the right, providing covering fire to the 2nd Section as it manoeuvred to attack WN-60 from the rear. While organising the attack Cutler noticed that the 1st Section, under Lt Kenneth E. Klenk, was in the process of assaulting the German trenches from the north-west corner of the position, using grenades and satchel charges to blast the Germans out. Cutler therefore called off his own attack, and having signalled 3/16th RCT that WN-60 had been captured, moved inland. In fact, the Germans claimed to have held on to part of WN-60, and mounted several counter-attacks from

Key (legend):
- ① Anti-tank ditches
- ② Easy-1 exit
- ③ Easy-3 exit
- ④ Fox-1 exit
- a Colleville-sur-Mer church
- Base map: IGN 1412OT

St-Laurent-sur-Mer

les Cosnes

Easy Red

Fox Green

Fox Red

le Révolution

WN-60

WN-61

le Cavey

le Moulins

WN-62

Village de Vacances

GR 223

WN-63

WN-64

WN-65

Cimetière militaire américain

Cabourg

le Robinson

la Fontaine

le Bray

la Mare au Tendeur

D514

D517

D51

St-Si

0   0.5   1

this area later in the day. Nevertheless, they were unable to close the F-1 draw to US troops moving inland.

While the attack on WN-60 has rightly been seen as critical for opening the draw, many histories of the fighting on Fox Green have ignored the vital attack made by a section from E/116th RCT and three sections from F/16th against WN-61, supported by tanks from 741st Tank Battalion. Their attack prevented WN-61 from bringing fire to bear against L/16th, and cleared the final block to movement off the beach up the Fox-1 draw.

The first blow against WN-61 was struck around 0710 hours when a DD Sherman tank commanded by Staff Sgt Sheppard disabled the 88-mm gun at WN-61. Following this, E/116th RCT's 6th Section opened a gap through the barbed wire with bangalore torpedoes, fired bazooka rounds at several German positions, then moved to outflank WN-61 from the east, reaching a location part-way up the bluffs. From here they knocked out a mortar position with rifle fire and grenades. Observing another attack into WN-61 from below by elements of F/16th RCT, and receiving orders from a Navy Shore Fire Control Party to retire from the bluff, 6th Section retraced its steps and then joined what had become a general move up the Fox-1

A view east along Fox Green and Red. The cliffs under which elements of 3/16th RCT took cover are clearly visible. Above the white buildings in the centre of the picture is the location of WN-60, with the Fox-1 draw to its right. *(TB)*

WN-61's 88-mm gun casemate, knocked out by Staff Sgt Sheppard's Sherman. *(TB)*

draw, involving elements of all the other companies that had landed on Fox Green.

F/16th RCT's assault against WN-61 was probably made by 4th and 5th Sections. Leading F/16th RCT's 5th Section, Technical Sgt Raymond F. Strojny used a bazooka to knock out several pillboxes and emplacements. Staff Sgt Piyo, commanding the 4th Section's mortar squad, also knocked out several positions. With his ammunition expended, he then led several men forward in an attack, which may have been the one observed from above by 6th Section, E/116th RCT.

Despite the successful assaults against WN-60 and WN-61, the Fox-1 draw was not opened until 2000 hours, when two tanks of B Company, 745th Tank Battalion, crested the hill via a road constructed by 336th Engineer Combat Battalion. The delay in opening the draw was caused by artillery fire forcing 336th ECB to land 4 km to the west of the Easy-3 draw. The battalion eventually reached Easy-3 by about 1730 hours. At the Fox-1 exit formal organisation was abandoned in preference for *ad hoc* teams, who started clearing routes through the shingle with a surviving tankdozer. A few mine detectors, built by cannibalising damaged units, were used to sweep ahead of the bulldozer as it cleared a road up the bluff. In the evening contact with A Company, 6th Beach Battalion, led to LCTs and other craft being sent to Fox Green in anticipation of the road being opened and it was briefly used for exit traffic on 6 June. In the following days, however, the steepness of the gradient meant that Fox-1 was re-designated only for return traffic to the beach.

STAND D2: WIDERSTANDSNEST 62

DIRECTIONS: Return to your vehicle and retrace the route to Colleville. About 100 metres from where the road forks, the one-way system takes you right, up the valley side. On the plateau following, you can park in the car park on the right where WN-62 is signposted. Alternatively, continue along the road as it turns south and follow the signs for the American Battle Monuments Commission Cemetery. Retrace your route on foot to WN-62. Please note that the cemetery gates close in late afternoon (time according to season). The car park nearer WN-62 does not close because it is outside the main grounds of the cemetery. Beside the car park at WN-62 is a map board showing the layout of the German positions. Follow the path down towards the beach, pausing at the 1st US Infantry Division Memorial, until you reach the 5th Engineer Special Brigade Memorial located on top of one of the two casemates that housed 75-mm anti-tank guns.

THE ACTION: Companies B and C, 741st Tank Battalion, were scheduled to land five minutes before H-Hour on Fox Green and Easy Red to cover the demolition teams and the first waves of 16th RCT. The rough sea conditions meant that only five out of 32 tanks made the shore, three of which were quickly knocked out by fire from WN-61 and WN-62. However, around 0630 hours, A Company and 741st Tank Battalion headquarters, landing direct from LCTs, did land successfully. These provided vital fire support to the infantry along the two beach sectors.

Privates Arthur Baker, John Froehlick and Charles D. Anderson, crewmen of an M4A4 Sherman tank from Headquarters Company, 741st Tank Battalion, related their experiences on Fox Green.

'Coming in the tank commander was shocked and would not give any order except to abandon tank. The loader couldn't load the gun so the bow gunner had to get into the turret and load the gun and command the tank. After we had hit the beach, we gave our blankets to the wounded and fed them. We gave our machine guns to the infantry to keep the snipers down while we were working. The tank was almost drowned out, so we had to drain the water and dry the motor. We pushed a bank of dirt up to shield the infantry. Sgt. Robert W. Compton came to our tank and did maintenance work for us. Pvt. Anderson asked him to

The 5th Engineer Special Brigade Memorial. The brigade's actions on 6 June earned it the French Croix de Guerre. *(TB)*

take his tank and help remove obstacles from the beach. He worked for three hours under fire. He proceeded to clear the beach of wooden obstacles, which had no mines attached to them, and to pull the obstacle element "C" back upon the beach and out of the way. All during this time, there was mortar, 88mm fire and sniper fire… '

Source: Combat interviews, HQ 3rd Armored Group, US National Archives.

Defending WN-62 were 22 men of 3rd Company, 726th Grenadier Regiment, and ten others drawn from 352nd Artillery and 916th Grenadier Regiments. Many of the troops were young and inexperienced; *Gefreiter* (Corporal) Franz Gockel was only 17 and had received only six weeks basic training. The unit was bolstered by a cadre of experienced NCOs who, assisted by the simple desire of the men to survive, managed to create a strong defence. The noise and dust of the preliminary bombardment of WN-62 made a strong impression on its defenders. When a shell burst close to *Gefreiter* Heinrich Severloh, delivering a violent blow to his steel helmet, he was impressed by the calm concern of *Oberleutnant* (Lt) Bernhard Frerking for his welfare. Others did not react so well to the pounding. Severloh saw *Wachtmeister* (Sgt) Fak crouching in cover, frozen with fear.

Most of the Allied fire landed to the rear, however, and WN-62's garrison suffered only a single casualty. As the men from two sections of F/16th RCT began disembarking they therefore came under accurate and sustained fire, causing them 50 per cent casualties crossing the beach. H/16th RCT, arriving 20 minutes late at 0730 hours, suffered similar losses. Gockel's attempt to halt the American advance was initially frustrated when his machine gun jammed. He managed to clear it, but the weapon was then sheared in two while in his hands by a large enemy round. Severloh developed a technique of first using his MG42 machine gun against large groups and then switching to his rifle for carefully-aimed shots at individuals.

Despite the ferocity of the defence the Germans also took losses and the upper 75-mm gun casemate was disabled. Some accounts say this was done by a DD tank at 0630 hours. However, according to F/16th RCT, no tanks arrived in the area until around 1030 hours, when they began to engage emplacements. Several tanks also tried to penetrate directly up the draw, but a concealed 50-mm gun commanded by *Obergefreiter* Siegfried Kuska knocked several out, halting the advance.

According to Severloh, German casualties mounted through the morning as Allied naval gunfire picked off German positions by locating the muzzle flashes of their weapons. This problem became particularly acute in the afternoon when ammunition shortages forced the defenders to start firing tracer rounds that easily revealed their positions. Several destroyers had concentrated about 800 metres offshore by the afternoon to support the American advance. The USS *Carmick* and *Frankford* are reported to have delivered heavy fire into German positions on the west of the Easy-3 draw, probably WN-62.

The result of this fire was the gradual erosion of the strength of WN-62's garrison. *Oberfeldwebel* (Sgt-Major) Schnüll was killed and *Oberfeldwebel* Pieh, commander of

The view from WN-62 on to Fox Green, looking down on the Easy-3 draw and towards WN-61 at the base of the opposite bluffs. *(SCT)*

LCI 83, which was hit off Fox Green at 0830 hours and unable to land men of 20th ECB, is shown finally disembarking its troops at around 1115 hours. (USNA)

3rd Company, 726th Regiment's men, was wounded. Both Severloh and Gockel were wounded.

Around 1400 hours, with no sign of the requested reinforcements or ammunition, and with US infantry clearly visible on the high ground to the west, Lt Frerking told Severloh that WN-62 was being abandoned. After assembling in a trench with seven other men, Severloh bolted towards Colleville under small arms fire. He reached the main coastal road with only one other man, the rest apparently having been killed; he was later taken prisoner here. Gockel was more fortunate, managing to reach transport near Colleville that took him to the rear. He was finally taken prisoner in the Vosges in November 1944.

STAND D3: THE AMERICAN CEMETERY

DIRECTIONS: There are two possible routes to this stand. For the first descend via the steep path from WN-62 to the car park at its base. To reach this location by vehicle drive along the one-way system from WN-62 or the cemetery to the roundabout at the D517 and repeat the route in Stand D1 to the beach via Colleville. This time take the left fork on the gravel road to the car park below WN-62. Go to the western side of the car park and take the path along the dunes. Walk west for some 500 metres until the cemetery's viewing platform overlooking the beach, and the path leading up to it, are visible on the bluff.

The second route involves parking in the cemetery. Walk through the main entrance and continue straight ahead along the path to reach the platform overlooking the beach. In wet weather the gently stepped path to the beach can be flooded, though there are benches half-way down from which the area of the assault up the bluff can be viewed, although WN-64 to the west is obscured by dense vegetation.

THE ACTION: Companies E and F, 16th RCT, were scheduled to land along Easy Red at 0630 hours. Most sections landed too far to the east and met heavy fire from WN-62. E/16th RCT's commander, Captain Edward F. Wozenski, noted that their heavy loads, the deep water and strong cross-currents meant that his men could only wade slowly towards the beach, exposing them for a substantial time. Despite the chaos and losses, once at the shingle bank Wozenski and his remaining officers and NCOs began to organise their men to return fire. Others bravely went back to the beach to drag wounded comrades to cover. There was no fire support or smoke to cover the company because most of the radios were lost or damaged. However, smoke from damaged landing craft, knocked-out tanks and the general haze of battle gradually provided a degree of cover for Wozenski and his men. Soon after, E/16th RCT began a move westward towards a yellow flare that was spotted on top of the bluff. This was the signal that someone had reached the top of the bluff.

Men of the Provisional Engineer Special Brigade, photographed by Robert Capa, take cover amongst obstacles on Easy Red as follow-up waves of landing craft approach, *circa* 0700 hours. (IWM AP25724)

Partial remains
of the WN-64
position, captured
by Lt Spalding
and Sgt Streczyk.
Both received
the Distinguished
Service Cross.
(DN)

Opposite: The
grave of Medal
of Honor winner
1st Lt Jimmie W.
Monteith, Jr., in
the American
National
Cemetery above
Omaha Beach.
(DN)

The unit responsible for breaching the bluff was Lt John N. Spalding's platoon of E/16th RCT. This unit had landed in F/16th RCT's sector towards the centre of the bluffs running from Easy 1 to Easy 3, with one section from F/16th RCT and two from E/116th RCT. Most accounts attribute the assault up the bluffs to Spalding's leadership, but it is clear from after-action reports, and interviews conducted many years later, that Technical Sgt Philip Streczyk led the first section of the platoon forward, with Spalding bringing up his section afterwards.

Furthermore, the attack by these sections was made with the support of Company G, 16th RCT, which landed around 0700 hours. Many of the men had become so cramped in the packed landing craft that they had to lie in the water rubbing their legs before they had the strength to crawl ashore. G/16th RCT's commander, Captain Joseph T. Dawson, quickly organised the setting-up of machine guns and mortars. When German fire shifted from their positions to the next waves approaching the shore, G/16th RCT's men were able to locate the German positions and open fire, though with mixed results. However, under cover of this fire, infantry and engineers were able to make the vital move forwards and blow the barbed wire ahead with bangalore torpedoes.

Streczyk advanced through one of the gaps blown by men of Company A , 37th ECB, covered by G/16th RCT's fire. A natural defilade with a path was used to ascend the bluff. At the top Streczyk's section, and possibly Spalding's, arrived beside an emplacement, which they assaulted with grenades and bazooka fire. Several defenders were killed and two, unable to flee with the rest of their comrades, were taken prisoner. Spalding then led his men west to WN-64, swiftly occupying an outer trench at the rear before the Germans were aware of their presence. Lacking

Above: Gen Montgomery decorates Sgt Streczyk of 16th RCT with the British Military Medal for his gallantry on 6 June. (IWM B6550)

the strength for a major assault, Spalding, Streczyk and the rest of their men fought in twos and threes for over 4½ hours. During this time they took 21 prisoners and killed a number of Germans. The final destruction of WN-64 was critical to completing the opening of the Easy-1 draw and the movement of reserves and vehicles off the beach.

During Streczyk and Spalding's assault, G/16th RCT had crossed the open ground at the base of the bluffs, avoiding mines by stepping on the bodies of those already killed, and then climbed up. Captain Dawson then led his men towards Colleville. The actions by Spalding's platoon and Dawson's company opened the first major route for the bulk of 16th RCT off Easy Red. Regimental commander Col George Taylor cajoled the men of A, B and C/16th RCT and any he found from other units to follow a similar route with the words, 'Two kinds of people are

A view of WN-64 from Easy Red. This position was assaulted from the rear by elements of E/16th RCT. Its neutralisation in mid-morning was vital in opening the Easy-1 draw. *(IWM HU87653)*

staying on the beach, the dead and those who are going to die – now let's get the hell out of here!'

ENDING THE TOUR: There is really only one way to complete this tour, or any visit to Omaha Beach, and that is to set aside time to pay one's respects in the American National Cemetery and Memorial.

Managed by the American Battle Monuments Commission, the 172-acre site was dedicated on 18 July 1956, having been donated without charge or tax by the people of France. Set within the extensive and immaculate grounds is an excellent Visitors' Building to the left of the main entrance. On the right is the semi-circular memorial, whose inner sides are engraved with stone maps of D-Day and the Normandy battle. In the centre is a 7-metre bronze statue depicting 'The Spirit of American Youth Rising from the Waves'. Behind the memorial is the Garden of the Missing on whose wall are inscribed the

AMERICAN NATIONAL CEMETERY AND MEMORIAL

For information:– tel: +33 (0)2 31 22 40 62; web: <www.abmc.gov>.
Open: Summer 0900–1800 (1000–1800 weekends and holidays)
              Winter 0900–1700 (1000–1700 weekends and holidays)
              Closed 25 December, 1 January.

names of 1,557 personnel with no known graves. There is also a non-denominational chapel.

Surrounding the chapel in carefully-organised plots are 9,386 white crosses or Stars of David. These include 307 unknown burials, four women and three Medal of Honor winners. The sight of the brilliant white headstones, laid in immaculate lines and set against the dark greens of the surrounding trees, is beautiful, moving and tragic. Carved on each headstone is the name, rank, unit, state, and date of death. Yet in a way this information does not make the person any less anonymous, or enable one fully to comprehend the nature of their death, let alone picture over 9,000 individual deaths.

The noted war correspondent Ernie Pyle, who visited Omaha Beach on 7 June (and was killed on the Pacific island of Okinawa in April 1945), wrote perceptively about what cemeteries like Colleville say to those of us who have never experienced battle and those who have.

'Dead Men by mass production – in one country after another – month after month and year after year. Dead men in winter and dead men in summer.

Dead men in such familiar promiscuity that they become monotonous.

Dead men in such monstrous infinity that you come almost to hate them.

These are the things that you at home need not even try to understand. To you at home they are columns of figures, or he is a near one who went away and just didn't come back. You didn't see him lying grotesque and pasty beside the gravel road in France.

We saw him, saw him by the multiple thousands. That's the difference… '

Source: Excerpt from an unfinished article 'On Victory in War', quoted in *Ernie's War: The Best of Ernie Pyle's World War II Dispatches*, ed. David Nichols, p. 419.

PART FOUR

ON YOUR RETURN

FURTHER RESEARCH

Most of the material for this book came from either published official sources or from documents in the US National Archives or the National Archives of Great Britain, or from published personal accounts. Of particular value were the combat interviews undertaken in 1944 and 1945 that formed the basis for the US Army official studies. But there is no shortage of books dealing with various aspects of the battle, and telling the stories of the men who fought it. The following were the most useful to the authors.

Operation 'Neptune': The Landings in Normandy 6th June 1944, British Naval Staff History Battle Summary Number 39, 1952; reprinted London, HMSO, 1994.

Omaha Beachhead; American Forces in Action Series, Historical Division, Department of the Army; Washington DC, The Center of Military History United States Army, 1945.

Small Unit Actions; American Forces in Action Series, Historical Division, Department of the Army; Washington DC, The Center of Military History United States Army, 1946.

Opposite A view of WN-65's 50-mm gun casemate after 6 June, when WN-65 was used by the Provisional Engineer Special Brigade Group, responsible for operating Omaha as a landing area for follow-up troops and logistics. *(USNA)*

Below: The memorial to the Rangers on the Pointe du Hoc. *(DN)*

Georges Bernage, *Omaha Beach, 6 Juin 1944*; Bayeux, Heimdal, 2001.

Joseph Balkoski, *Beyond the Beachhead: The 29th Infantry Division in Normandy*; Mechanicsburg PA, Stackpole, 1989.

Joseph Balkoski, *Omaha Beach: D-Day June 6, 1944*, Stackpole Books, Mechanicsburg, 2004

Richard T. Bass, *The Brigades of Neptune: US Army Engineer Special Brigades in Normandy*; Lee Publishing, Exeter, 1994.

Joseph Binkoski and Arthur Plaut, *The 115th Infantry Regiment in World War II*; Washington DC, Infantry Journal Press, 1948.

David Chandler and James Lawton Collins (eds.) *The D-Day Encyclopedia;* New York, Simon and Schuster, 1994.

Alain Chazette, *Le Mur de l'Atlantique en Normandie*; Bayeux, Heimdal, 2001.

Joseph H. Ewing, *29 Let's Go! A History of the 29th Infantry Division in World War II*; Washington DC, Infantry Journal Press, 1948.

Francis Douglas Fane and Don Moore, *The Naked Warriors*; London, Allan Wingate, 1957.

Jonathan Gawne, *Spearheading D-Day: American Special Units of the Normandy Invasion*; Paris, Histoire & Collections, 2001.

Gordon A. Harrison, *Cross Channel Attack*, United States Army in World War II, The European Theater of Operations; Washington DC, The Center of Military History United States Army, 1951.

David C. Isby (ed.), *Fighting in Normandy: The German Army from D-Day to Villers-Bocage*; London, Greenhill, 2001.

David C. Isby (ed.), *Fighting the Invasion: The German Army at D-Day*; London, Greenhill, 2000.

Alex Kershaw, *The Bedford Boys: One Small Town's D-Day Sacrifice*; London, Simon & Schuster, 2003.

Robert J. Kershaw, *D-Day: Piercing the Atlantic Wall*; Shepperton, Ian Allan, 1993.

Tim Kilvert-Jones, *Omaha Beach: V Corps's Battle for the Normandy Beachhead*, Barnsley, Leo Cooper, 1999.

H.R. Knickerbocker *et al.*, *Danger Forward: The Story of the First Division in World War II*, Washington, Zenger, 1979.

Adrian R. Lewis, *Omaha Beach: A Flawed Victory*; Chapel Hill, University of North Carolina Press, 2001.

Samuel Eliot Morison, *The Invasion of France and Germany 1944–1945*; History of United States Naval Operations in World War II; New York, Little, Brown, 1957.

David Nichols (ed.), *Ernie's War: The Best of Ernie Pyle's World War II Dispatches*, New York, Random House, 1986.

Cornelius Ryan, *The Longest Day: The D-Day Story*; London, Victor Gollancz, 1982.

Anthony Saunders, *Hitler's Atlantic Wall*; Thrupp, Sutton, 2001.

William White (ed.), *By-Line: Ernest Hemingway*, London, 1968.

Theodore A. Wilson (ed.), *D-Day 1944*; Abilene KA, University Press of Kansas, 1971.

Steven J Zaloga, *Rangers Lead the Way: Pointe du Hoc D-Day 1944*, Osprey Publishing, Oxford 2004

Niklas Zetterling, *Normandy 1944: German Military Organisation, Combat Power and Organizational Effectiveness*; Winnipeg, J.J. Federowicz, Winnipeg, 2000.

Most of these books would be available only from specialist libraries or through inter-library loan. In Great Britain, good starting places for any study of D-Day and the battle of Normandy are the Imperial War Museum, and the D-Day Museum at Southsea near Portsmouth.

USEFUL ADDRESSES

UK National Archives, Public Record Office, Kew, Richmond, Surrey TW9 4DU; tel: 020 8876 3444; web: <www.nationalarchives.gov.uk>.

US National Archives, The National Archives and Records Administration, 8601 Adelphi Road, College Park, Maryland MD 20740-6001; tel: +01 866 272 6272; web: <www.archives.gov>.

Imperial War Museum, Lambeth Road, London SE1 6HZ; tel: 020 7416 5320; web: <www.iwm.org.uk>.

D–Day Museum and Overlord Embroidery, Clarence Esplanade, Southsea PO5 3NT; tel: 023 9282 7261; web: <www.ddaymuseum.co.uk>

British Library, 96 Euston Road, London NW1 2DB; tel: 020 7412 7676; web: <www.bl.uk>.

The Aerial Reconnaissance Archives (TARA) [formerly University of Keele Air Photo Library], The National Collection of Aerial Photography, RCAHMS, John Sinclair House, 16 Bernard Terrace, Edinburgh, EH8 9NX; tel: 0131 662 1456; web: <http://aerial.rcahms.gov.uk>.

INDEX

Page numbers in *italics* denote an illustration.